# THE FRAGILITY OF ORDER

GEORGE WEIGEL

# The Fragility of Order

*Catholic Reflections on*
*Turbulent Times*

IGNATIUS PRESS    SAN FRANCISCO

Cover art:
*Fall of the Rebel Angels*
Pieter Bruegel the Elder, 1562

Cover design by John Herreid

FOR
+BORYS GUDZIAK
AND
+ROBERT BARRON

# CONTENTS

## Part Three

### The Church in the Postmodern World

# INTRODUCTION

## *Things Coming Apart?*

Not so long ago, Irish poet William Butler Yeats' often-quoted lament about things falling apart and mere anarchy being loosed upon the world seemed rather exaggerated. Take the summer of 1991, for example.

On August 15, 1991, the Soviet Union disintegrated—remarkably, on the liturgical feast of the Assumption of the Blessed Virgin Mary, celebrated the same day by both the Christian East and the Christian West. Two years earlier, during what history now knows as the Revolution of 1989, the Soviet external empire built by Lenin and Stalin self-liberated, led by Poland. Between 1989 and 1991, independence movements in the Baltic states, led by Lithuania, began dismantling the "Union of Soviet Socialist Republics": Lenin's and Stalin's internal empire. The coup de grâce for the entire Soviet enterprise, arguably the greatest tyranny in human history, came when a hardline revolt against Soviet president Mikhail Gorbachev failed and the "republics" of the Soviet Union one by one detached themselves from the USSR's Russian core.

And at that point, the Great Emergency ended: the civilizational crisis that began in 1914 and threatened to destroy the West (and, in its latter phases, the entire world) seemed to have been resolved in favor of the forces of freedom. Imperfect democracies had defeated a pluperfect tyranny; a "third wave" of democratization seemed poised to sweep the globe; free economies, unshackled from socialist-bureaucratic control, would liberate the world from gross poverty and deliver unprecedented wealth; new forms of international and transnational political organization, linking free societies in a thick network of collaborative efforts, would replace the old power games of world politics; "peace with honor", which

9

British prime minister Neville Chamberlain so vainly proclaimed in 1938, was at hand.

As for the United States, the blood and treasure it had invested in the Cold War seemed vindicated. America was the dynamo of world-historical initiative. Deft American diplomacy led to the reunification of Germany and the creation of what looked to be a permanently stable, peaceful, and wealthy Europe. More creative diplomacy produced a major drawdown of nuclear weapons. A prominent intellectual proclaimed it the "end of history", and the American people imagined that they could begin to enjoy a long-sought peace dividend, even as their high-tech military proved itself capable of maintaining the rudiments of a new world order in the First Gulf War.

While the world seemed on the brink of a new era of peace and prosperity, the Catholic Church—the world's largest religious body, which had proven itself a powerful agent of liberation in the Revolution of 1989—seemed ready to provide this post–Cold War world with a compelling moral compass, even as it felt itself reenergized for its primary mission: the conversion of the world.

A brilliant pope, John Paul II, had ignited the revolution of conscience that made the nonviolent, political Revolution of 1989 possible. On May 1, 1991, he issued a striking encyclical, *Centesimus Annus*. Originally conceived as a centennial commemoration of Pope Leo XIII's seminal 1891 social encyclical, *Rerum Novarum*, the stirring events in Europe throughout the 1980s led John Paul II to write *Centesimus Annus* as a prescription for the future—a future of freedom in which democratic politics and market-centered economies, guided by law and tempered by a vibrant public moral culture, would shape the human future in ways consonant with the inalienable dignity and value of every human being. Four years later, John Paul put that vision before the General Assembly of the United Nations, boldly claiming that the "tears of [the twentieth] century [had] prepared the ground for a new springtime of the human spirit."

And the Church would contribute to that springtime by recovering its original self-understanding as a communion of missionary disciples. Thus, shortly before *Centesimus Annus*, on December 7, 1990, John Paul II issued another landmark encyclical, *Redemptoris Missio* (The Mission of the Redeemer). There, he taught that the Church did not *have* a mission, as if "mission" were one of a dozen things the Church did; rather, the Church *is* a mission, and everyone in the Church is a missionary, commissioned by baptism to help spread the Gospel throughout the world. Shortly afterward, John Paul began using the term "the New Evangelization" to express this contemporary recovery of the Church's original purpose. Then, in drawing the Great Jubilee of 2000 to a close, the Pope challenged the entire Catholic world to leave the shallow waters of institutional maintenance and "put out into the deep" for a great catch of souls, following the Lord's injunction in Luke 5:4 that led to the miraculous draught of fish.

A world poised to achieve all the great things imagined before World War I because order had been restored to global affairs after the seventy-seven years of the Great Emergency; an America imagining itself returned to the natural order of things, at peace with the world and beginning to feel the expansive economic effects of the IT revolution; a Church eager to offer humanity the healing truth of the Gospel and to make its unique contribution to building free and virtuous societies, because it had rediscovered its own "order" and purpose—it was a heady time indeed.

A quarter-century later, things look rather different. In fact, on the edge of the third decade of the twenty-first century and the third millennium, Yeats' premonition of things coming unraveled seems increasingly prescient—in the world, in the American republic, and in the Church. And to continue to borrow images from the Irish poet, it is not at all certain what the many rude beasts slouching toward Bethlehem portend about the future of Catholicism, America, or the world. Order, it has become clear, is a very fragile thing; and order is especially vulnerable under the cultural conditions of a postmodern world unsure about its grasp on the truth of anything. Order is not self-maintaining. Order is an achievement, and it must be attained, over and again.

This is perhaps most obvious in terms of world affairs. If peace, as Saint Augustine taught, is the "tranquillity of order", the "order-dividend" that might have been expected at the end of the Cold War turned out to be something of a chimera. The unfinished business of the First Gulf War was followed by the lethal crack-up of Yugoslavia, which was followed by largely ignored signals that jihadist Islam had the West, and particularly the United States, in its apocalyptic crosshairs—a fact that became unmistakably clear on September 11, 2001. That cataclysmic event led to wars in Afghanistan and Iraq, a debilitating world-weariness on the part of the American people, the reassertion of Russian power by a virtual dictator who never got the memo that the Cold War was over, a newly aggressive China flexing its muscles throughout East Asia, and so forth and so on, in a litany of disorder that seemed inconceivable in 1991—and that seemed ominously intractable a quarter-century later.

Order also rapidly unraveled in the United States: first, moral order, as the acids of postmodernist skepticism and relativism worked their way through the population; then, cultural order, as what philosopher Ernest Fortin once dubbed "debonair nihilism" became the default position in both high and popular culture; finally, political order. Solidity of character was no longer deemed a minimum prerequisite for high public office. Partisanship intensified, not least at the points where moral judgment and public policy intersected. Finally, in 2016, the country embarrassed itself before the world in a presidential campaign of unprecedented vulgarity.

As for the Church, the assumption that the pontificates of John Paul II and Benedict XVI had restored a sufficient measure of order—understood as evangelical purpose—after the upheavals of the post-Vatican II period was dramatically falsified by the quick (and in some instances, cheerful) resumption of intra-Catholic conflict during the first years of Pope Francis. In the apostolic exhortation *Evangelii Gaudium* (The Joy of the Gospel), the Argentine pope declared a Church "permanently in a state of mission" the hope of his heart and the grand strategy of his pontificate, in a line of continuity with John Paul II's New Evangelization. But Francis seemed unpersuaded by the claim, and the evidence, that the living, evangelically dynamic parts of the world Church were those that had embraced Catholicism in full, and that the dying parts of the Church were those in thrall to "Catholic Lite". The result, exemplified by the Synods of 2014 and 2015 and the raucous global debate over the post-synodal apostolic exhortation *Amoris Laetitia* (The Joy of Love), was not an intensification of missionary fervor but a deterioration into discord and disunity.

The essays collected here, originally written over the past two decades, have been revised for this volume. Each attempts to analyze one or another aspect of the unraveling that so many sense in these first decades of the third millennium; some even propose first steps toward a resolution of that unraveling. But the primary concern here is one of diagnosis, not prescription.

These reflections may seem, at first blush, to cover a lot of disconnected, noncontiguous territory. The common thread among them is the twinned conviction that has animated my thought and work as a theologian at the crossroads of moral reasoning and public life. The first conviction is that both American democracy and the future of freedom in the world are jeopardized when the deep truths inscribed into the world and into us by what the American Founders called in the Declaration of Independence "the Laws of Nature and of Nature's God" are ignored—or worse, dismissed as irrational prejudice. The related, or twinned, conviction is that it is the Church's task, through its evangelical mission and its witness in the public square, to teach and embody those deep truths, both for the healing of broken humanity and to provide some sort of grammar for an orderly public debate over the human future.

In turbulent times, the Christian does well to keep in mind that, however much mankind may be making a mess of things, the truth announced by the Lord when he first sent the Twelve out on mission remains the truth: "The kingdom of heaven is at hand" (Mt 10:7). And while the Church may feel itself buffeted by the cultural exhaust fumes of a West now reckoning with the grave intellectual and moral damage it suffered before and during the Great Emergency, Catholics should also remember that deep spiritual and moral conviction can leverage change for the better. In *Lumen Gentium* 9, writing at a more optimistic moment, the Fathers of the Second Vatican Council nonetheless offered the Church of this moment an important lesson when they described the nature of the Church and its place in the world in these stirring terms:

"Behold the days shall come saith the Lord, and I will make a new covenant with the House of Israel, and with the house of Judah.... I will give my law in their bowels, and I will write it in their heart, and I will be their God, and they shall be my people.... For all of them shall know Me, from the least of them even to the greatest, saith the Lord" (Jer. 31:31–34). Christ instituted this new covenant, the new testament, that is to say, in His blood (cf. 1 Cor. 11:25), calling together a people made up of Jew and gentile, making them one, not according to the flesh but in the Spirit. This was to be the new People of God. For those who believe in Christ, who are reborn not from a perishable but from an imperishable seed through the word of the living God (cf. 1 Pt. 1:23), not from the flesh but from water and the Holy Spirit (cf. Jn. 3:5–6), are finally established as "a chosen race, a royal priesthood, a holy nation, a purchased people ... who in times past were not a people, but are now the people of God" (1 Pt. 2:9–10)....

So it is that that messianic people, although it does not actually include all men, and at times may look like a small flock, is nonetheless a lasting and sure seed of unity, hope and salvation for the whole human race. Established by Christ as a communion of life, charity and truth, it is also used by Him as an instrument for the redemption of all, and is sent forth into the whole world as the light of the world and the salt of the earth (cf. Mt. 5:13–16).

Those who believe that to be the truth may have cause for concern about the state of affairs in the world, the American republic, and the Church. But believing that to be the truth, they have no cause for despair, and they have no choice but to put out into the deep in a mission of truth-telling, healing, and conversion.

# Part One

# A World without Order

# The Great War Revisited

## Why It Began, Why It Continued, and What That Means for Today

In 1936, the British writer Rebecca West stood on the balcony of Sarajevo's town hall and said to her husband, "I shall never be able to understand how it happened." "It" was World War I—the civilizational cataclysm that began, according to conventional chronology, when Archduke Franz Ferdinand, heir to the throne of Austria-Hungary, was assassinated in the Bosnian capital on June 28, 1914, by Gavrilo Princip, a twenty-year-old Bosnian Serb.

World War I was known for decades as the "Great War". It seems an apt title. For if we think of a century as an epoch rather than an aggregation of one hundred years, what we know as "the twentieth century" began with the guns of August 1914 and ended when one of the Great War's consequential by-products, the Soviet Union, disintegrated in August 1991. World War I set in motion virtually all the dynamics that were responsible for shaping world history and culture in those seventy-seven years: the collapse of dynastic power in the fall of the German, Austro-Hungarian, Russian, and Ottoman empires; the end of the Caliphate; new nation-states, new tensions in colonial competition, and new passions for decolonization; the mid-twentieth-century totalitarianisms; efforts to achieve global governance; the next two world wars (World War II and the Cold War); the emergence of the United States as leader of the West; serious alterations in the basic structures of domestic and international finance; and throughout Western culture, a vast jettisoning of traditional restraints in virtually every field, from personal and social behavior to women's roles to the arts.

It was the "Great War" in other ways, too. History had never seen such effusive bloodletting: twenty million dead, military and civilian,

17

with another twenty-one million wounded and maimed. Beyond that, the Great War created the conditions for the influenza pandemic that began in the war's final year and eventually claimed more than twice as many lives as were lost in combat.

Sixty-five million soldiers, sailors, and airmen were called to their respective national colors in a struggle that evoked great acts of valor. Between 1914 and 1918, more than six hundred Victoria Crosses were awarded to British and Dominion troops. In Australia, Anzac gallantry during the 1915 Gallipoli campaign is still remembered as *the* formative experience of Australian nationhood. The names Sergeant York and Eddie Rickenbacker, both World War I Medal of Honor recipients, continue to inspire courage among Americans.

The Great War also raised profound moral questions about war, nationalism, and prudence in political and military affairs. It was the war during which the idea that "the great and the good" governed society by natural birthright was buried; the war in which the British poet Wilfred Owen, awarded the Military Cross for heroism in combat, wrote that those who had experienced a gas attack "would not tell with such zest / To children ardent for some desperate glory / The old Lie: *Dulce et decorum est / Pro patria mori*". Owen and the other British antiwar poets were not alone in thinking that something had gone badly awry between 1914 and 1918. No less enthusiastic a warrior than Winston Churchill could write, in the war's aftermath, that "all the horrors of all the ages were brought together, and not only armies but whole populations were thrust into the midst of them.... Neither peoples nor rulers drew the line at any deed which they thought could help them to win.... Europe and large parts of Asia and Africa became one vast battlefield on which after years of struggle not armies but nations broke and ran."

These jarring juxtapositions—between a young fanatic's terrorist act in provincial Sarajevo and the global carnage that followed; between inspiring episodes of extraordinary heroism and a debilitating sense of civilizational guilt that things had ever come to such a pass—have shaped interpretations of the Great War for a century. At one hermeneutic pole, the war is regarded as a virtually incomprehensible act of civilizational suicide. That conclusion, first shaped by the failures of the postwar Versailles Treaty to restore order in

Europe, by the antiwar writings of poets like Owen and Siegfried Sassoon, and by German novelist Erich Maria Remarque in *All Quiet on the Western Front*, was later accepted by such eminent historians as Britain's Lewis Namier (who called World War I "the greatest disaster in European history") and Columbia University's Fritz Stern (for whom the Great War was "the first calamity of the twentieth century ... from which all the other calamities sprang"). At the other pole of judgment, the Great War was a necessary piece of nasty work that prevented a militaristic, authoritarian Germany from dominating Europe politically and economically.

Nor has a firm consensus been established on who started the Great War, or, to put it another way, why it all happened in the first place. In wrestling with that elusive question, the twenty-first-century student of the Great War may actually be aided by our twenty-first-century fondness for using "narrative" as an analytic tool. Thus Cambridge historian Christopher Clark usefully reminds us that, in seeking to understand how such a cataclysm could have begun, we must reckon with the fact that all the key actors in our story filtered the world through narratives that were built from pieces of experience glued together with fears, projections, and interests masquerading as maxims. In Austria, the story of a nation of youthful bandits and regicides (i.e., Serbia) endlessly provoking a patient elderly neighbor got in the way of a coolheaded assessment of how to manage relations with Belgrade. In Serbia, fantasies of victimhood and oppression by a rapacious, all-powerful Habsburg Empire did the same in reverse. In Germany, a dark vision of future invasions and partitions bedeviled decision-making in the summer of 1914. And the Russian saga of repeated humiliations at the hands of the Central Powers had a similar impact, at once distorting the past while seeming to clarify the present. Most important of all was the widely trafficked narrative of Austria-Hungary's historically inevitable decline, which disinhibited Vienna's enemies, undermining the notion that Austria-Hungary, like every other great power, possessed interests that it had the right to defend.

To which one could add: the French nightmare of a demographically more robust Germany completing the absorption of Alsace and Lorraine, achieving European economic supremacy, and rendering France incapable of defending itself unaided; the classic British grand strategy of preventing any one power from achieving hegemony in continental Europe; Italian fantasies of revived Roman glory; American indifference to European politics; Japanese colonial ambitions in European-dominated Asia; and a number of other incompatible, and thus dangerous, narratives.

A century into the debate over causation, one suspects that the question of why the Great War happened will never be finally settled. Perhaps, though, it is time to consider a different question, rarely explored but no less urgent: Why did the Great War *continue*? Why, at the end of 1914, when the military situation had ossified on both the Western and Eastern fronts, did Europe find it impossible to call a halt? As the train of European civilization careened toward the edge of a cliff, why was Europe unable to recognize impending disaster and find a different path toward the future? Why, as Aleksandr Solzhenitsyn put it in his 1983 Templeton Prize Lecture, did Europe, "bursting with health and abundance", fall into "a rage of self-mutilation that could not but sap its strength for a century or more, and perhaps forever"?

Thinking about these questions may shed more light on the crises of our civilization and the challenges of statecraft in the twenty-first century than would devising an all-purpose explanation for how the war began in the first place. Yet there are lessons to be learned from recent attempts to deal with that question, so serious reflection on the Great War rightly begins there.

Contemporary considerations of how the war began start from the premise that there is more than enough blame to go around. Indeed, a close reading of the historical record provides sobering insights into the follies of which statesmen are capable—follies even more shocking when one considers the seeming placidity of European life in early 1914. Here was a continent accustomed to disarmament conferences and international arbitration, where men and women traveled freely, without passports; a continent in which ancient enemies France and Germany seemed to have entered a period of stable relations; a continent of unprecedented wealth that was the undisputed center of world affairs. Yet within a little over five weeks, it all unraveled.

The survey of miscreants can begin with Serbia. For while the Great War was not "caused" by the assassination of Franz Ferdinand

in Sarajevo, Gavrilo Princip's shots, fired in aid of Serbian irreden-
tism, did set in motion the chain of events that eventually led the
guns of August to erupt across the continent.

From the mid-nineteenth century on, Serbian national identity
centered on a passion to gather all Serbs into a single state. But because
Serbian historical resentments and future ambitions did not easily fit
the demographic and political realities of the Balkans, a culture of
deception, embodied in clandestine political societies and violent
conspiracies, came to play a disproportionately large role in Serbian
politics, eventually laying the ideological and logistical foundations
for the deadly events of June 28, 1914. And as Serbia was drawn
into the tangled web of alliances that France, fearful of Germany,
was weaving throughout Central and Eastern Europe, the encouragement of Serbian adventurism by Russia, self-appointed tutor of
the Slavic peoples, reinforced Greater Serbia radicals in their impression that the Habsburg Empire would soon unravel, with Pan-Serb
redemption to follow.

Then there was Austria-Hungary. Walking through central Vienna
today, one cannot help being struck by the cornerstones of the city's
splendid public buildings, many of which bear dates from the early
twentieth century. The wheels were about to come flying off the
venerable Habsburg Empire, yet no one seemed to know it; Vienna
was building for an imperial future that was a phantasm.

In 1914, that false sense of enduring Habsburg solidity was embodied in the emperor Franz Joseph, who had been on the throne since
1848. The empire's incapacities and fractiousness, by contrast, were
displayed in its ramshackle political structure, in which the two dominant ethnic groups, Germans and Hungarians, shared power over a
hodgepodge of restive peoples, each of which had been developing
its own national consciousness throughout the nineteenth century.
The net result was the curious combination of durability and res-
tiveness that led Viennese journalist Karl Kraus to wisecrack that the
Austrian situation was always "desperate, but not serious".

But Kraus' joke eventually fell flat. It was not widespread public
outrage over the assassination of the Austro-Hungarian heir and his
consort that brought the Habsburg Empire to war; Franz Ferdinand
had been unpopular in Viennese governing circles and throughout
the empire. Rather, war came because of the determination of the

Dual Monarchy's political and military leadership to buttress Austria-Hungary's hold over the southern Habsburg lands, using the Sarajevo murders as the excuse for the war they had long wanted to fight against the advocates of Greater Serbia. Yet eager as they were to take on the Serbs, the dithering of Vienna's policy makers and military leaders, compounded by Berlin's irresponsibility in underwriting Austrian incompetence with a blank-check guarantee of support, was a major factor in helping turn what might have been another local Balkan fracas into a continental conflagration.

As for Germany, the political fall of Otto von Bismarck, who had assembled the German Empire in "blood and iron", ironically helped pave the way toward a general European war. Bismarck worried that "the great European war will come out of some damned foolish thing in the Balkans", but he also thought preventive war to forestall Russian hegemony in southeastern Europe an idiocy. After dismissing the Iron Chancellor in 1890, Kaiser Wilhelm II reversed Bismarck's alliance policies, brushed off Russia, and encouraged a belligerent Austro-Hungarian policy in the Balkans, thus setting the stage for Russia's alliance with France. Concurrently, Wilhelm decided to challenge British naval supremacy by building his own oceangoing fleet, which in turn accelerated British efforts to come to terms with ancient foe France, now bound to Russia.

Wilhelm's personal volatility was another factor in the diplomatic and political death spiral that began in July 1914. Yet, prior to those fatal weeks, it was Wilhelm who, in yet another historical irony, typically came down on the side of peace when decisions had to be made. Thus, in March 1914, the Austro-Hungarian chief of staff, Franz Conrad von Hötzendorf, was told by the German ambassador in Vienna that there would be no war of the sort Conrad sought against Serbia and Russia, because "two important people are against it, your Archduke Franz Ferdinand and my Kaiser". In the aftermath of the assassination of his friend, the Habsburg heir, however, Wilhelm pivoted again and gave Austria-Hungary what amounted to an absolute guarantee of German support—a guarantee that, whether Wilhelm recognized it or not, made a general war virtually inevitable, as Russia would think itself obliged to come to Serbia's aid, France was bound to support Russia (and thus go to war with Germany), and Britain, newly reconciled to France and long committed to permitting no hegemon on the continent, would find it difficult to remain aloof.

Wilhelm was not the only irresponsible party in Germany, however. The German chief of staff, Helmuth von Moltke, thought war with Russia inevitable and wanted to fight it sooner rather than later. The German chancellor, Theobald von Bethmann Hollweg, miscalculated the likelihood of Russia's going to war for Serbia, even as the kaiser miscalculated his personal influence on Tsar Nicholas II. Both chancellor and kaiser miscalculated the effects of their blank check to Austria-Hungary as it was formulating its post-assassination ultimatum to Serbia (which Serbia swallowed hard and, essentially, accepted). The German military leadership, and conservative German political circles, saw a general European war as a nation-rallying opportunity to stem what they perceived as a rising tide of social democracy, thereby reasserting both traditional authority and the kind of fierce nationalism that social democrats were thought (wrongly, it turned out) to reject as a matter of internationalist conviction.

Nor were the German and Austrian governments entirely honest with each other. Austria claimed to be punishing Serbia for the Sarajevo assassinations, when the assassinations were the excuse for the punitive war Austria had long sought against its turbulent Balkan neighbor. The Germans promised to keep Russia and France at bay in the confidence that they would never have to do so, thus issuing a blank check they thought would not be cashed. The military men in the Central Powers were equally unforthcoming. Austrian chief of staff Conrad expected Moltke to handle the Russians while the Austro-Hungarians put paid to Serbia. Moltke, however, did not share with Conrad the German general staff's determination to fight a holding action in the East while striking what they believed would be the decisive blow at France through Belgium—a stratagem that left the incompetent Austro-Hungarian military in the lurch and virtually ensured British entry into the war, given British guarantees of Belgian neutrality.

The net result of all this folly is neatly summed up by historian David Fromkin, who noted that, as of August 4, 1914, Germany "was fighting Russia, France, Britain, Luxemburg, and Belgium—all supposedly to prop up Austria, which, as of August 4, was still at peace with all of them. Yet Germany was *not* at war with, or fighting against, Serbia, the only country with which Austria *was* at war and which, according to Vienna, was the country that posed the threat to Austria's existence."

Russian, French, and British stupidities also loom large in understanding the Great War's origins. Nikolai Hartwig, Russia's minister in Belgrade from 1909 until his death during the July 1914 crisis, was a militant Pan-Slavist who encouraged Serbian aggressiveness in the half-decade before the Great War. Russian policy in the crucial last days of July 1914 was also driven by the conviction that a Russian failure to stand by Serbia at all costs would be lethal to Russia's role as leader of the Slavs. Thus Pan-Slavic ideology helped shape the fateful Russian decision to be the first great power to declare general mobilization, from which much followed.

French folly lay in a diplomacy that offered Russia a Gallic version of the German blank check to Austria, and in a military theory of the offensive that combined ignorance of the new technological realities of war with a gross misreading of German strategy, thus creating the military conditions for the possibility of the Western Front stalemate that lasted from late 1914 until late 1918.

And then there was Great Britain. Few remember today that, when the bullet from Gavrilo Princip's Browning semiautomatic hit Franz Ferdinand's jugular vein, the United Kingdom was in political disarray, with parliament bitterly divided over women's suffrage, labor unrest, and the budget. Even worse, the UK was on the brink of civil war in Ireland, with armed Ulstermen preparing to defy Irish Home Rule and the British Army on the verge of mass mutiny. Amid this domestic turmoil, the two British statesmen most responsible for foreign affairs, Prime Minister Herbert Asquith and Foreign Secretary Sir Edward Grey, were slow to grasp the dangerous reality of the situation after the deaths in Sarajevo. On July 9, Grey still saw "no reason for taking a pessimistic view of the situation". Twenty days later, Asquith wrote his confidant, Venetia Stanley, that attending an Army Council on July 29 was "rather interesting, because it enables one to realize what are the first steps in an actual war".

The "actual war", of course, began a few days later. And Britain entered it, not after a parliamentary vote or any consultation with the Dominion governments or parliaments, but after an August 3 speech in the House of Commons by a now-chastened Sir Edward Grey, making the case for British intervention in defense of Belgian neutrality against a German invasion. A British ultimatum to Germany followed and was ignored. Thus what might have been a regional conflict, and had already become a continental conflict, became a global one.

Although this multiplicity of follies is telling, it would be a mistake to conclude that World War I began because of a sequence of accidents, for the leaders of the great powers uniformly believed they were rational actors pursuing attainable political objectives. That sense of rationality and rectitude was reinforced by the various national "mythscapes" previously alluded to. Churchill may have written his wife on the night of July 28, bemoaning the "wave of madness which has swept the mind of Christendom", just as German chief of staff Moltke could warn his government a day later that, in the event of war, "the civilized states of Europe will begin to tear one another to pieces" in a conflict that would "annihilate the civilization of almost the whole of Europe for decades to come". Yet, in the event, both Moltke and Churchill were prepared to risk that annihilation, given the "mythscapes" within which they made their decisions.

During the war itself, rationales for fighting shifted, even as continuities in grand strategy—Germany's determination to preserve Austria-Hungary as a great power; Britain's determination to save France and prevent German continental hegemony; Austria-Hungary's determination to save itself as a multinational empire—played themselves out. Still, the ebb and flow between changing rationales for prosecuting the war, on the one hand, and consistent grand strategic goals, on the other, do not get us to the root of the question of why the Great War *continued*.

By the end of 1914, it was clear on both the Western and Eastern fronts that a war of maneuver resulting in quick victory was impossible. The First Battle of the Marne and the First Battle of Ypres had frustrated Germany's strategy in the West. Austrian incapacities in the East, plus the seemingly limitless availability of human cannon fodder for the tsar's armies, had made it impossible for the kaiser's forces to follow up on their victory at Tannenberg in late August 1914 and drive Russia out of the war. A war of attrition—a vast bloodletting in which the last nations standing, however shakily, would be the "victors"—now seemed inevitable. (Churchill, recognizing that strategic impasse and its lethal implications, proposed the Dardanelles Campaign in 1915 precisely to break out of the gridlock that was bleeding Europe to death.)

Thus British military historian Max Hastings argues that, as awful as the situation was by the end of 1914, there was nothing for the Western allies to do but carry on, until a combination of German exhaustion, American manpower, and the power of the tank broke the stalemate in the West (Russia having been driven from the war by the Bolshevik seizure of power in the fall of 1917). "Until 1918," Hastings writes, "the fundamental options before the western allies were those of acquiescing in German hegemony on the continent, or of continuing to bear the ghastly cost of resisting this. It was, and remains, a huge delusion to suppose that a third path existed."

But even if Hastings is right, the question still remains, why was *that* the case? Why were leaders who entered the war for what they understood to be rational purposes unable to find a path beyond the irrationality of civilizational suicide, something that seemed more than merely possible as early as January 1915? Some answers can be found in the various "mythscapes" that shaped national identities and aspirations in Europe in 1914, and in the more tangible, if incommensurable, vital interests for which leaders believed themselves to be expending their country's manhood. Yet one should probe deeper into the cultural subsoil of late nineteenth- and early twentieth-century European life in pursuing the question of why the Great War continued. For beneath the surface of a seemingly placid and prosperous continent were distorted ideas and virulent passions that help account for the otherwise inexplicable, or at least deeply puzzling, lack of some "third path".

There was Charles Darwin's theory of evolution, which, it seems, had an effect not only on science and religion but on politics as well, as the survival of the fittest came to be understood as the victory of the most lethal rather than the triumph of the best adapted. That misconception of evolutionary theory as a scientific justification for the fierce arms races that preceded the Great War fit readily into a moral-cultural environment that had been profoundly influenced by Friedrich Nietzsche—by his irrationalism, his proclamation of the death of God, his notion of regeneration through destruction, and, perhaps above all, his celebration of the will to power.

Nietzsche's Prometheanism could take many forms, including radical political willfulness. Marry such willfulness to a mindless faith in technology, and the outcome was something unprecedentedly lethal. A new order of magnitude in military capabilities was not complemented by a parallel development in strategic and tactical wisdom; military leaders tried to compensate with ever greater exertions of will; those exertions produced ever greater numbers of casualties, which were then interpreted as evidence of a willingness to endure greater suffering and loss. (Nietzsche was not the only problem here. Henri Bergson's theory of *élan vital* as the driver of human development helped shape the French army's passion for the offensive, which almost cost France its national life when, in the late summer of 1914, General Joseph Joffre's Plan XVII ran into the hard truth that men's chests are ill-fitted to stopping machine-gun bullets.)

Xenophobia and national-racial theories also played a large and destructive role in prewar European high culture and politics. These irrationalities, and the instability and murderousness to which they could lead, were obvious in the Balkan hinterlands, but the great powers were not immune to the racial, eugenic, and ethnic toxins of the age. Although Kaiser Wilhelm II and Tsar Nicholas II exchanged "Willy and Nicky" letters for years, beneath the surface bonhomie in the monarchs' guild there were deeper and uglier convictions in play—convictions about the ultimate incompatibility of Teuton and Slav that shifted perceptions of war, as the classic great power calculations of men like German chancellor Bismarck and British prime minister Salisbury a generation earlier were supplanted by images of an inevitable racial struggle to the death.

The dark view of the future of the early twentieth-century German ruling class—expressed in the kaiser's 1912 warning that Germany would "have to fight this racial war" if necessary to save Austria's position in the Balkans—found its mirror image in the Pan-Slavism that was a powerful factor in Russian governmental and diplomatic circles. German contempt for Russians and Russian resentment of German achievements seemed, in Berlin and Saint Petersburg, to have been vindicated by the brief Balkan Wars of 1912 and 1913. Thus minor regional conflicts were understood as confirmation that a racially fated continental death struggle was near at hand. We may think, today, that no such racial Armageddon was inevitable. But German and Russian fatalism about the inevitability of a race-based general European conflict went some distance in bringing that very conflict about.

Social Darwinism, Nietzschean irrationalism, xenophobia, and historical fatalism were acids eating away at notions of honor that had long tempered European politics and war making. For concepts of honor must be informed by prudence, the cardinal virtue the ancients called the "charioteer of the virtues", lest honor become an excuse for cruelty rather than a restraint on it. And as Churchill would later write, there was little restraint shown by any of the combatants in the Great War:

> Germany, having let Hell loose, kept well in the vanguard of terror; but she was followed step by step by the desperate and ultimately avenging nations she had assailed. Every outrage against humanity or international law was repaid by reprisals often on a grander scale and longer duration.... The wounded died between the lines: the dead mouldered into the soil. Merchant ships and neutral ships and hospital ships were sunk on the seas and all aboard left to their fate, or killed as they swam. Every effort was made to starve whole nations into submission without regard to age or sex. Cities and monuments were smashed by artillery. Bombs from the air were cast down indiscriminately. Poison gas in many forms stifled and seared the soldiers.... When it was all over, Torture and Cannibalism were the only two expedients that the civilized, scientific, Christian States had been able to deny themselves: and these were of doubtful utility.

The complex process that Owen Chadwick described in his 1973–1974 Gifford Lectures as the nineteenth-century "secularization of the European mind" surely played its role in all this—and especially in the erosion of any sense of rules or restraint in world politics or the conduct of war.

In the Europe of 1914, biblical understandings of the human condition and the moral life had been under assault for well over a century, from both within and without the churches. From without, Auguste Comte's positivism (empirical science is humanity's only reliable teacher), Ludwig Feuerbach's subjectivism (the biblical God is a mere projection of human aspiration), and Karl Marx's materialism (the spiritual world is an illusion) meshed with Nietzsche's will to power to erode any biblically or theologically informed understanding of public life and political responsibility. From within, the more radical forms of historical criticism of the Bible and what was then known as liberal theology had, many thought, emptied the Christian creed of serious intellectual content. Evacuated of substance, the churches that professed those creeds and read that Bible became ever more expressions of ethnic and national consciousness—a process exacerbated by the subordination of many European Christian churches to state power through the mechanism of religious establishment.

Add to all this the anticlericalism that shaped class consciousness among rapidly secularizing European workers during the Industrial Revolution, and the strange forms of neo-paganism that surfaced in European high culture in the latter half of the nineteenth century, and one can begin to understand that, while millions of German soldiers went into battle wearing army-issue belts with buckles bearing the inscription *Gott mit uns* (God with us), the God in question had little to do with the God of the Bible and his moral injunctions—as witness the actions of those Bavarian infantry, presumably including pious Catholics, who in 1914 razed the village of Dahlin in Lorraine and shot its priest for his supposedly French sympathies.

The effects of this century-long assault on the Christian worldview can also be detected among churchmen who, like many others, drank deeply from the wells of a nationalism that seemed beyond the reach of Christian moral critique. Thus when the College of Cardinals met in September 1914 to elect a successor to Pope Pius X (an acute analyst of the signs of the times who repeatedly predicted a *guerrone*—a terrible war, or, literally, "great war"), the German cardinal Felix von Hartmann said to the Belgian cardinal Désiré Mercier, "I hope that we shall not speak of war," to which Mercier shot back, "And I hope that we shall not speak of peace."

A German chaplain put it even more vehemently to the troops he addressed: "Rage over Germany, you great holy war of freedom. Tear down all that is rotten and sick, heal the wounds on the body of our German people and let a breed grow, a new breed, full of reverence for God, faithfulness to duty, and brotherly love." The Catholic bishop of the Austrian diocese of Seckau got matters exactly backwards when he celebrated the outbreak of war as "the end of culture without God, without Christ, [and of] high politics without religion". But his fervor was mild compared to that of the German pastor who cast the war in explicit, if debased, theological terms: "It is a hard task that you are called upon to undertake, but one that is essential to your people's salvation. Even amid death and destruction you can become wonderful evangelists for idealism." Or the Anglican bishop of London, who urged his congregants to "kill Germans: kill them, not for the sake of killing, but to save the world; to kill the good as well as the bad. . . . As I have said a thousand times, [this is] a war for purity." Given such pious rodomontade, is it any wonder that an apocalyptic-messianic distortion of nationalism became evident in virtually all the countries that fought the Great War?

What Max Weber famously described as a disenchanted world turned out to be a terribly dangerous world. The Religion of Humanity found itself unable to check ancient racial animosities, tarted up in the fancy dress of modern eugenic and racial theories, and emboldened by a Promethean will to power that legitimated lurid forms of nationalism in which the national Other was thoroughly dehumanized. Thus the disenchanted world led to inhumanity on an unprecedented scale in the Great War—and then gave birth to even greater horrors in Communism and German National Socialism.

According to one account of European history, modern forms of political authority arose to end the slaughters caused by competing religious authorities during and after the Reformation. Whatever truth there is in that telling of the tale, it should also be recognized that the erosion of religious authority in Europe over the centuries—meaning the erosion of biblically informed concepts of the human person, human communities, human origins, and human destiny—created a European moral-cultural environment in which politics was no longer bound and constrained by a higher authority operative in the minds and consciences of leaders and populations.

Some will doubtless think it too simple to suggest that the most penetrating answer to these grave questions—Why did the Great War begin, and why did the Great War continue?—is the answer suggested by Aleksandr Solzhenitsyn three decades ago: it was because "men [had] forgotten God." Yet just as the political follies that led to war in the late summer of 1914 bear lessons for the twenty-first century—such as the necessity of taking seriously the "mythscapes" within which others live, however fantastic or irrational they may seem to us, and the impossibility of the great powers that stand for order in the world remaining idle while the forces of disorder gather strength—so do the moral-cultural conditions that underwrote the Great War and its continuation.

The European world that went to war in 1914—the world that may yet prove to have bled itself of civilizational vitality in the Great War—was one in which the masters of the world's leading civilization believed they could create a humane future without the God of the Bible. What they proved, however, was that they could only build a world against each other, which was a world with no future.

# Through a Glass, but More Clearly

## Ten Principles for Renewing the American Debate on Morality and Foreign Policy

The debate over morality and foreign policy is at least twenty-four hundred years old, as we learn from reading the "Melian Dialogue" in Thucydides' *History of the Peloponnesian War*. In the modern American context, and counting from the presidencies of Theodore Roosevelt and Woodrow Wilson, that debate has careened through at least ten cycles, resulting in numerous, and sometimes jarring, shifts in the American approach to the world. The starting point for this to-and-fro coincided with the Great War, as the years from 1914 to 1920 witnessed the emergence, the peak, and the collapse of Wilsonian idealism—an internationalism quite self-conscious in its moral assertiveness, which distinguished it from the robust Realpolitik internationalism of Theodore Roosevelt.

The most memorable expression of that idealism came in Wilson's April 1917 war message to Congress, in which the president declared that America's aim in entering the conflagration then consuming Europe was to ensure that the world would be "made safe for democracy". That such noble sentiments could coexist with a curious political fastidiousness, bordering on prissiness, is evident in a less-remembered formulation of President Wilson's—that his interventions throughout the Caribbean and in Mexico during his first term in the White House were intended "to teach the South American republics to elect good men". Like Teddy Roosevelt's Realpolitik internationalism, Wilsonian idealism was shaped by notions of Anglo-Saxon cultural superiority that contemporary progressives, Wilson's political heirs, would find more than a little embarrassing.

In the immediate aftermath of the "war to end all wars", Wilsonian idealism was displaced by the "normalcy" of Warren G.

Harding and the rise of a strong isolationist current in American politics—a tide of public opinion so formidable that even as strong and crafty a president as Franklin Delano Roosevelt was compelled to tack carefully across it, even as he prepared the United States for its inevitable entry into World War II. American isolationism in those days was a curious business, finding lodgments across the spectrum of political opinion. But whether it was the by-product of Burton K. Wheeler's progressivist politics, Joseph P. Kennedy's Anglophobia, Charles A. Lindbergh's racial and eugenic speculations, or Robert A. Taft's business-oriented conservatism, isolationism was thought to be finished as a serious force in American public life after December 7, 1941.

The national consensus born at Pearl Harbor was strong enough to permit President Harry Truman, working with Secretaries of State George Marshall and Dean Acheson, and such Republican leaders as Arthur Vandenberg, John Foster Dulles, and Dwight D. Eisenhower, to define and execute a vigilant and interventionist internationalism that continued through the Eisenhower, Kennedy, and Johnson administrations (albeit with different strategic and tactical accents, articulated in different registers of moral passion). Although not without its idealist elements, the analytic starting point of this form of internationalism was a realist assessment of the mid-twentieth-century situation: totalitarianism was a mortal peril to free societies, and resisting its aggressive encroachments required the United States to take the lead in defense of the West, since Europe had unmanned itself in the two midcentury world wars.

Such leadership would take American power into lands about which Americans previously knew very little. Still, and notwithstanding considerable costs in blood and treasure, the creators of the postwar internationalist consensus also thought it *vere dignum et iustum*, "truly right and just" as the Roman Missal says, that the United States take such a leading role in world politics, for, on balance and considering the alternatives, American power was a positive force in the world. The prudent exercise of American power was not only necessary but *good*, for it aimed at securing the morally worthy goal of peace through freedom. The rhetorical proclamation of that conviction reached its apogee in President Kennedy's inaugural address of January 20, 1961:

Let the word go forth from this time and place, to friend and foe alike, that the torch has been passed to a new generation of Americans— born in this century, tempered by war, disciplined by a hard and bitter peace, proud of our ancient heritage—and unwilling to witness or permit the slow undoing of those human rights to which this nation has always been committed, and to which we are committed today at home and around the world.

Let every nation know, whether it wishes us well or ill, that we shall pay any price, bear any burden, meet any hardship, support any friend, oppose any foe to assure the survival and the success of liberty.

Within five years of President Kennedy's assassination in 1963, however, the postwar internationalist consensus disintegrated and isolationism reemerged as a powerful force in American public life— not an isolationism fearful of America becoming contaminated by the world but the isolationism of the New Left, convinced that America itself was a poison in and for the world. This new isolationism (which was far more moralistic than anything it found objectionable in the rhetoric of John Foster Dulles) quickly swept up the Democratic Party, such that, a mere eleven years after Kennedy's inaugural, the Democratic candidate for president of the United States was urging America to "come home" and being cheered on in that neo-isolationism by the late president's youngest brother and others who claimed JFK's political mantle.

Meanwhile, the Republican Party under Richard Nixon and Henry Kissinger had adopted a self-consciously realist approach to world politics, drawing on such contemporary intellectual sources as Hans Morgenthau and Albert Wohlstetter and such European historical models as the diplomacy of Metternich and Disraeli. In its pursuit of détente with what some realists judged to be an ascendant Soviet Union, the realism of the Nixon-Ford years downplayed, for instance, human rights violations behind the Iron Curtain. Yet the Ford administration also negotiated the Basket Three human rights provisions of the 1975 Helsinki Final Act, which turned out to be a powerful weapon in the hands of human rights activists throughout the Warsaw Pact countries in the endgame of the Cold War.

In response to the realism of the Nixon-Ford years, a new, morally urgent human rights activism was born in the mid-1970s within those elements of the Democratic Party aligned with Senator Henry M. Jackson, including pro-democracy social democrats and the trade-union movement. After Jimmy Carter defeated Jackson for the 1976 Democratic presidential nomination and bested President Ford in the subsequent general election, the Carter administration adopted the language of an assertive human rights policy but filled it with New Left content, aiming its criticism primarily at authoritarian American allies rather than at America's totalitarian enemies. President Carter's announcement at Notre Dame in 1977 that Americans had gotten over their "inordinate fear of communism"—together with Secretary of State Cyrus Vance's statement that Carter and Soviet leader Leonid Brezhnev shared "similar dreams and aspirations about the most fundamental issues"—demonstrated that a meltdown of moral judgment into moral posturing could coexist with breathtaking strategic myopia (and indeed moral blindness) in minds for which the evocation of the specter of Vietnam marked an end to moral reasoning, or indeed any other form of reasoning.

Ronald Reagan challenged the realism of the Nixon and Ford administrations in 1976, but without articulating an alternative strategic vision that drew on the human rights themes being developed by the Jackson wing of the Democratic Party. That had changed by 1980, thanks in part to the work of Jeane J. Kirkpatrick, Norman Podhoretz, Carl Gershman, Elliott Abrams, and others; their intellectual and policy advocacy filled out the contours of Reagan's longstanding anti-Communism by adding to it the concept of an America once again acting as the international champion of liberty, on the model of Kennedy's inaugural. The election of Pope John Paul II and his triumphant visit to Poland in June 1979 accelerated Reagan's sense that the Soviet emperor had fewer clothes than the realists imagined and deepened his conviction that the Cold War might actually be won, not simply managed.

The Revolution of 1989 in Central and Eastern Europe—an epic series of events ignited by moral passion, informed by moral conviction, sustained by deft and morally sophisticated politics, and supported by a resolute demonstration that the Soviet Union could not compete with the United States in a serious arms race—raised further questions about classic foreign policy realism and its narrow focus on "hard power" as the sole analytic prism for understanding both the dynamics of world politics and the exigencies of American foreign policy. Nonetheless, the administration of George H. W. Bush restored something of a realist perspective to the White House, through the work of Secretary of State James A. Baker III and national-security adviser Brent Scowcroft. This more conventional approach to the world successfully managed the endgame of the Cold War while effecting the reunification of Germany; it proved far less capable of managing the genocidal dissolution of Yugoslavia or seeing off Saddam Hussein in Iraq.

Then came the Clinton years, during which America took something of a holiday from history—and from serious thought about the relation between ideals and realities, moral norms and prudential judgments, in formulating and executing foreign policy. Staffed primarily by veterans of the Carter administration, whose views had first been shaped by the shattering of liberal nerve that forged the McGovernite consensus about Vietnam, the Clinton administration seemed content to rely on a dumbed-down version of Francis Fukuyama's argument that history had in fact ended with the triumph of democracy and the free economy in the collapse of European Communism between 1989 and 1991. In truth, of course, this blindness to enduring realities and new, lethal challenges was shared across a wide swath of the American foreign policy community of both parties. Where it could lead was made unmistakably clear on September 11, 2001, after previous signals about history's implacable turbulence had been insufficiently understood when they erupted in Kenya, Tanzania, and Aden.

President George W. Bush had come to office in January 2001 promising a modest approach to America's engagement with the world, but the September 11 cataclysm compelled his administration to a profound reexamination of the premises of foreign policy, particularly with reference to the despotic regimes in the Middle East from which so much of the world's turmoil emerged. Having gone into both Afghanistan and Iraq with the full force of American might, Bush dedicated his second inaugural address, in January 2005, to articulating a "Freedom Agenda" that, in its premises, mirrored John Paul II's 1995 address to the United Nations, and, in its moral passion and political scope, was no less breathtaking than the Kennedy inaugural:

We are led, by events and common sense, to one conclusion: The survival of liberty in our land increasingly depends on the success of liberty in other lands. The best hope for peace in our world is the expansion of freedom in all the world.

America's vital interests and deepest beliefs are now one. From the day of our founding, we have proclaimed that every man and woman on this Earth has rights and dignity and matchless value, because they bear the image of the Maker of heaven and Earth. Across the generations we have proclaimed the imperative of self-government, because no one is fit to be a master and no one deserves to be a slave. Advancing these ideals is the mission that created our Nation. It is the honorable achievement of our fathers. Now, it is the urgent requirement of our Nation's security and the calling of our time.

So it is the policy of the United States to seek and support the growth of democratic movements and institutions in every nation and culture, with the ultimate goal of ending tyranny in our world.

This forthright idealism led in time to another turn of the wheel, in which the customary positions of foreign policy idealism and realism got themselves inverted on the map of American politics. For in reaction to the difficulties of Bush's second term, and informed by the New Left themes that corrupted the strategic perceptions of the Carter and Clinton administrations, President Barack Obama's administration spent much of its first year in office proclaiming a "new realism" in foreign policy—a strange hybrid that saw the administration decline to defend human rights activists in Russia, China, and Iran, apologize for the suffering allegedly caused by American exceptionalism, turn its back on several key allies, and retool human rights to stress "reproductive choice" and what Secretary of State Hillary Rodham Clinton called the imperative of people being "free ... to love in the way they choose". Events subsequently forced the Obama administration to temper some of its "realism", but the general theme of retreat from obligations to others (sometimes packaged as "nation-building at home") remained intact—except for the administration's use of foreign aid dollars to promote the LGBT agenda aggressively in traditional societies.

Between Woodrow Wilson and Barack Obama, then, American foreign policy seems to have averaged one major shift in perspective every 9.5 years, changes influenced both by events in the world and by domestic political exigencies. These shifts have been jarring, but not (yet) fatal, for, in most cases, the American people and their leaders have usually ended up doing what they ought to have done, thus validating Winston Churchill's observation that the Americans will always do the right thing, after they've tried everything else. Nonetheless, oscillations between the idealist and realist poles of the debate over national interest and national purpose create significant difficulties, both within our own political culture and for the world. And thus it is important to understand their sources, with an eye to setting a steadier course.

These pendular swings have also been shaped by a defective understanding of how moral truths bear on world politics. At the risk of offending ecumenical proprieties, one significant part of our problem can be defined in these terms: this nation of high moral expectation and deep moral commitments has never had an adequate public philosophy for translating moral truths into a framework for strategic analysis and prudent foreign policy decision-making—and it has lacked such a public philosophy because the American debate over morality and foreign policy has been dominated by one form or another of an inadequate account of morality that derives from the left wing of the Reformation and its adoption of an Ockhamite, or voluntarist, notion of the moral life.

As John Courtney Murray pointed out in the late 1950s, this Protestant way of conceiving the moral life did not find good and evil in the moral structure God built into the world and into us—a structure we could discern by reason—but in the will of God alone. Good is *good* because God commands it; evil is *evil* because God forbids it. The notion of moral *reason* finds little purchase here, because reason is untrustworthy and capable of being the tool of passions or interests, both of which are Bad Things.

This Protestant concept of morality also tended to be biblicist, imagining that conclusions about complex issues of public policy could be derived without much exegetical ado from, say, the Sermon on the Mount or Saint Paul's injunctions on obedience to the public authorities (a perennial temptation to which some of the more vociferous evangelical Protestant supporters of President Donald Trump regularly succumb). It set a high value on motive or intention, was not much concerned with an analysis of possible consequences (the purity of the actor's will being what most counted), and thus was chary of the idea of a "national interest". As for society, including the passions and interests at play in the world, the individualism endemic to this understanding of morality often led to a curiously apolitical view of public policy: there would be no policy conundra, at home or abroad, if all men would just observe the second Great Commandment (or its secular equivalents).

This was the moralism that dominated American Protestantism in the first half of the twentieth century and that gave rise, by way of reaction, to the Neo-Orthodoxy of the Niebuhr brothers, on the one hand, and to the foreign policy realism of Hans Morgenthau and his school on the other. But Neo-Orthodoxy, despite its powerful critique of moralism and its trenchant reading of the moral obligations of public authority in the face of the totalitarianism threat, had no solution to the more basic problem of moral reasoning. For it, too, rejected or ignored the classic morality of right reason, substituting for what it found objectionable in the old liberal Protestant moralism such categories as "paradox" or "ambiguity", all the while trying to maintain its equilibrium in the unresolvable tension between moral man and immoral society.

Similarly, the realism of Morgenthau and his school provided no escape from America's cyclical oscillations between idealism and realism. Realism proved incapable of crafting an adequate analytic lens for reading the signs of the times in the last two decades of the Cold War: both liberal realists (such as those in the "arms-control community") and conservative realists missed the dynamics of conscience that made possible the Revolution of 1989. And realism missed those dynamics because its notion of the relation between moral truth and world politics—embodied in Hans Morgenthau's histrionic claim that "to know with despair that the political act is inevitably evil, and to act nonetheless, is moral courage"—was as defective as the moralism it criticized.

If we are to escape the past century's pattern of an America lurching between an idealism and a realism imagined to be two horns of a dilemma, when they are in fact two dimensions of a single problem, the United States needs a new template for thinking about the national interest and the national purpose. Such a template would give due

weight to the defense of the national interest as an inescapable responsibility of government. Yet it would also recognize that securing
the national interest must be located within the more ample horizon
of a national aspiration to advance what John XXIII in the April 11,
1963, encyclical *Pacem in Terris* called the "universal common good"—
the pursuit, on the international plane, of the five rationally knowable ends of any morally serious politics: justice, freedom, security,
the general welfare, and the peace of order. What follows, then, is
an intellectual grid for disciplining the American public moral debate
in the twenty-first century about the goods to be sought in world
politics and the means appropriate to the pursuit of those goods.

*1. There is no escape from moral reasoning in politics.* Politics,
even world politics, inevitably engages questions of good and evil:
what is noble and what is base, what is congruent with the truths we
can know to be true and what is incongruent with those truths. Thus
politics, as Aristotle and much of the classic Western philosophical
tradition have long affirmed, is an extension of ethics. This is obviously true of the politics of our domestic affairs; it is also true of world
politics, if in a distinctive way. Attempts to subtract or bracket the
moral dimension of politics from our calculus of ends and means in
the formulation and execution of foreign policy debases public life,
warps strategy, and leads to imprudent tactics.

*2. History can be bent to reason and will—to the human capacity
to know the good, to choose it, and to act on it.* Those who deny the
possibility of purposefulness in this kind of world, by appeals either to
"complexity" or to the "impersonal dynamics of history", have not
reflected very carefully on modern history. The twentieth century
was replete with examples of purposeful men bending history to their
will: Lenin, Hitler, Mao, and Ho Chi Minh among the odious examples; Churchill, the founders of the State of Israel, Reagan, Thatcher,
and John Paul II among the admirable examples. In the admirable
cases as in the odious ones, concepts of purpose were informed and
tempered by issues of interest. Interest and purpose thus seem to be
linked, empirically. And this linkage has something of the appearance
of a dialectic, in which interest and purpose interact and are thereby
mutually refined.

*3. The two twentieth-century forms of American moralism are both
antithetical to clear thought about the national interest and the national*

*purpose and thus weaken serious statecraft.* The traditional, culturally transmitted Protestant understanding of morality in America—voluntarist, subjectivist, biblicist, and individualist—is inadequate to the moral reasoning and practical action required of statesmen. Its suspicions about the idea of a national interest, like its discomfort with the exercise of power, render it a less than useful counselor to those responsible for the common good, who must try to drive principles into the hard soil of reality while taking care to safeguard the security of those whom they serve.

The secularist moralism that characterized the Vietnam-era New Left and shaped foreign policy in the Carter, Clinton, and Obama administrations—which looked rather like the old liberal Protestant moralism with God and the Bible tossed overboard—is also inadequate to the tasks of statecraft in the twenty-first-century world. Its ideological distortions preclude seeing things as they are, which is the essential prerequisite to wise policy. For we cannot advance toward how things ought to be if we do not grasp the nature of things as they are.

*4. Neo-Orthodoxy's critique of the older American moralism remains important in devising wise policy in the twenty-first century.* The moral sensibility articulated in the pre–World War II Protestant Neo-Orthodox critique of twentieth-century American Protestant moralism was defined by several imperatives: understanding the inevitable irony, pathos, and tragedy embedded in history; being alert to the dangers of unintended consequences; maintaining a robust skepticism about all schemes of human perfection (especially those in which politics is the instrument of salvation); appreciating democracy without worshipping it. These elements of the Neo-Orthodox or Niebuhrian sensibility remain essential intellectual furnishing for anyone who would think wisely about interest and purpose in foreign policy.

In the twenty-first century, however, the Christian realist critique of the older American moralism will be less a comprehensive framework and more an important set of cautions essential to the exercise of practical reasoning about America's action in the world, especially in light of the cyclical returns of New Left moralism and nationalist isolationism.

*5. Realist conceptions of world politics and foreign policy must be completed by a concept of human creativity in history.* Paying close attention to the cautions raised by the realist critique of the older American Protestant moralism and its New Left–influenced successor ought not lead to a form of intellectual paralysis in which the strategist and policy maker simply accept things as they are. Rather, any genuine realism, and certainly any genuine Christian realism, must guard against premature closure in its thinking about the possibilities of human action in this world. Things can change—things can be *made* to change—for the better. Sometimes.

*6. Social ethics, including that subset of social ethics known as "ethics and international affairs", is a distinctive moral discipline.* The moral reasoning appropriate to foreign policy will reflect the distinctive nature of political action. As John Courtney Murray put it, the obligations of society and the state are "not coextensive with the wider and higher range of obligations that rest upon the human person (not to speak of the Christian)". And thus "the morality proper to the life and action of society and the state is not univocally the morality of personal life, or even of familial life.... The effort to bring the organized action of politics and the practical art of statecraft under the control of the Christian values that govern personal and familial life is inherently fallacious. It makes wreckage not only of public policy but of morality itself."

This is a crucial point missed by the old Protestant moralism, New Left moralism, and the approaches to political theology sketched in recent decades by Stanley Hauerwas and representatives of the Radical Orthodoxy school. The moral reasoning appropriate to foreign policy will not apply moral norms appropriate to interpersonal relationships to world politics in a simple-minded, one-to-one correspondence. Rather, the moral reasoning we need will demonstrate to the statesman and policy maker that our choices are not between an immoral or amoral Realpolitik, on the one hand, and naïveté, on the other; international outlaws are not to be dealt with as one would deal with refractory children, nor are international negotiations exercises in therapy or pastoral accompaniment.

By the same token, the moral reasoning we need will keep statesmen and policy makers alert to the possibilities of nudging history in a more humane direction through a variety of means, by keeping public authority's attention focused on the imperative of pursuing the rationally knowable "universal common good" in our engagement with the world.

*7. It is in the American national interest to defend and enlarge the sphere of order in international public life, through prudent efforts at changing what can be changed in the trajectory and conduct of world politics.* The irreducible core of the American national interest is composed of those basic security concerns to which responsible public authorities must attend. Those security concerns are not unrelated to a larger sense of national purpose, however—we defend America because America is worth defending, in itself and because of what it means for the world. The security concerns that make up the core of the national interest should not be conceived in classic Realpolitik terms; rather, they should be understood as the necessary inner dynamic of the pursuit of the national purpose.

And the larger American purpose in world affairs is to contribute as best we can to the long, hard, never to be fully realized domestication of international public life: to the quest for ordered freedom in an evolving structure of international public life, capable of advancing the classic goals of politics (justice, freedom, security, the general welfare, the peace of order). As a matter of hard fact and as a matter of moral truth, the United States cannot adequately defend its national interest without seeking concurrently to advance these goals in the world. As a matter of hard fact and as a matter of moral truth, those goals will not be advanced when they are pursued in ways that gravely threaten the security of the United States.

*8. National purpose is not national messianism.* The national purpose is a horizon of aspiration toward which our policy (and our polity) should strive. That horizon of purpose helps us measure the gap between things as they are and things as they ought to be, even as it provides an orientation for the long haul. But "national purpose" as defined above is not something that can be achieved in any final sense, because international public life will never be fully domesticated, save under a particularly stringent global tyranny. Understanding national purpose as an orienting horizon of aspiration is a barrier against the cynicism that is the shadow side of realism, and, at the same time, a barrier against the dangers of a moralistic, even messianic, notion of national mission, which implies a far shorter timeline and the possibility of final accomplishment.

*9. Casuistry is the moral art appropriate to international statecraft.* For both the moral analyst and the policy maker, the relation between national interest and national purpose in the practical order is defined through casuistry: the moral art of applying principles to world politics by means of the mediating virtue of prudence. Prudence does not necessarily guarantee wise policy. Prudence does, however, reduce the danger of stupid policy based on moralistic or Realpolitik confusions.

The classic casuistry most in need of renovation in early twenty-first-century thinking about morality and foreign policy is the just-war tradition, which must be revitalized as a tradition of collaborative reflection on the nature of sovereignty, and on the legitimate sovereign's use of proportionate and discriminate armed force in the pursuit of peace. Conceptions of the just-war tradition that begin with a prima facie "presumption against war" and that conceive the tradition as a set of hurdles for statesmen to jump through are less than helpful in shaping the kind of reflection required by both the tradition of reason and wise statecraft.

*10. The debate over national interest and national purpose is perennial, but not necessarily circular.* The dialectic of interest and purpose will remain unresolved. Pursuing a narrow concept of interest without reference to purpose risks crackpot realism. Pursuing grand and noble purposes without regard for safeguarding the national interest risks crackpot idealism, or utopianism. The world being what it is, the temptations of crackpot realism and crackpot idealism may be unavoidable. Succumbing to those temptations is not unavoidable, however, given a clear understanding of the inherently moral character of political choice and the distinctive canons and methods of moral reasoning in the sphere of world politics.

Thus the debate over the right relation between the American national interest and the American national purpose will be a perennial one, given the nature of politics itself as well as the historical character of the American people and their democracy. If it is informed, however, by a proper understanding of the moral reasoning appropriate to thinking about world politics, the argument will not be circular and may yield a measure of wisdom from time to time.

Indeed, had such a template to discipline and guide the foreign policy debate been in place in the twentieth century, America might have helped craft a more just and sensible peace settlement after World War I, thus making the rise of National Socialist totalitarianism less likely; America might have found ways to prevent the Soviet absorption of half of Europe after World War II; America might not have abandoned its commitments and its allies in Southeast Asia, thus preventing the bloodbath that followed our withdrawal from the region; America might not have mistaken the threat posed by the ayatollah Ruhollah Khomeini, described by President Carter's U.N. ambassador as "some kind of saint"; America might have helped prevent genocide in the Balkans; and America might not have made such a hash of the post–major combat phases of the Gulf War and the Iraq War.

In politics, as in all things in history, we see through a glass darkly. But the opaqueness can sometimes be broken by the clarity of moral vision that comes from a correct understanding of the nature of morality and of moral reasoning. That understanding is what has often been missing in the American debate over the national interest and the national purpose.

Realist appeals to national interest often assume that we know, intuitively, what that interest is. But we do not. As Charles Frankel, a liberal with some sense, once put it, "The heart of the decision-making process ... is not the finding of the best means to serve a national interest already perfectly known and understood. It is the determining of that interest: the reassessment of the nation's resources, needs, commitments, traditions, and political and cultural horizons—in short, its calendar of values."

Determining the content of the national interest, and the means appropriate to its pursuit, is an exercise in moral reasoning and not merely a political-economic calculation. Therefore, the public debate in America ought to reflect a correct idea of what moral reasoning is and of how the moral reasoning peculiar to international politics functions. The failure to define and culturally instantiate such an idea of moral reasoning is at the heart of our oscillation between foreign policy idealism and foreign policy realism.

It is past time for both realists and idealists to recognize that they share a common tendency to reduce morality to something akin to the injunctions of the Sermon on the Mount. The idealists then seek to apply the dominical counsels—poverty of spirit, meekness, mercy, purity of heart—to the business of dealing with everyone from the Dalai Lama to Vladimir Putin and Kim Jong-un. The realists, agreeing that these dominical counsels sum up morality, insist that they cannot be applied to states or nonstate actors in world politics, concluding that foreign policy is the realm of amorality. Both camps assume that everyone agrees on what morality is and that the real arguments are about the possible or impossible application of that morality to world affairs.

That shared assumption is wrong. As a political culture, the United States has never really grasped what moral reasoning in foreign policy means and entails. The morality we need in foreign policy is one whose principles are derived from reflection on the ends of politics as these can be known by reason and whose practices are mediated through the virtue of prudence: the moral craft of applying principle to circumstance so as to maximize the chances of doing good and minimize the dangers of making things worse than they already are. This kind of moral analysis, rooted in the tradition of reason, does not easily yield simple answers. It is, however, the kind of moral reasoning appropriate to the distinctive vocation of the statesman and to the creation of a serious public conversation about the national interest and the national purpose.

Were all of this to be well understood, the oscillation between the idealist and realist poles of American foreign policy would abate, and the future of American foreign policy could be placed on a more steady course—which would be a good thing, for us and for the world.

# All War, All the Time

## *Lessons from the Communist Assault on the Church*

Martyrdom has been an integral part of Christian life since the Acts of the Apostles. Yet to many Christian minds, "martyrdom" is imaginatively confined to first-century Christianity: a matter of Richard Burton and Jean Simmons defying Jay Robinson's Caligula while Michael Rennie (Saint Peter) looks on paternally and a chorus of "Hallelujahs" brings *The Robe* to a glorious Hollywood conclusion. This, however, is a serious misconception of the history and geography of martyrdom. Modern totalitarianism caused an effusion of blood *in odium fidei* (in hatred of the faith) that was orders of magnitude greater than anything experienced before. The Commission for New Martyrs of the Great Jubilee of 2000 concluded that there were likely twice as many martyrs in the twentieth century as there were in the previous nineteen centuries of Christian history combined.

The great majority of these twentieth-century martyrs gave their lives for Christ at the hands of Communist regimes. Thanks to the new political situation behind the old Iron Curtain, it is now possible to unlock some of the most closely held secrets of this almost-forgotten Communist war against Catholicism and to describe the various methods of this lethal assault on the Church in detail. For this was an undercover war as well as a matter of mass murder: it involved spies and spymasters, moles and agents of influence, propaganda, disinformation, and other "active measures", just as it did slave labor camps and the bullet in the back of the head.

Since the Communist crack-up in 1989–1991, serious research has been conducted in what remains of the archives of Communist-era governments and secret police organizations in Berlin, Warsaw, Budapest, and Prague, and even briefly in Moscow. Thus in the last

decade of the twentieth century and the first decades of the twenty-
first, scholars have been able to "eavesdrop" on East German spymaster Markus Wolf and Yuri Andropov, chairman of the Soviet
secret intelligence service, the KGB, as they speculated on the threat
posed by the 1978 election of a Polish pope, speculations shaped by
the reports of Communist Bloc moles inside the Vatican. Research-
ers have likewise been able to "sit in" on negotiations between the
Polish Communist government and the Holy See on the terms and
conditions of John Paul's second pastoral visit to his homeland, even
as they have been able to "watch" an effort by the *Służba Bezpie-
czeństwa* (or SB, the Polish secret police) to influence those negotiations by trying to blackmail the Pope. These newly available materials also shed light on Vatican diplomacy's efforts to find a modus
vivendi with Communist governments, even as those governments
were intensifying their efforts to penetrate the Vatican.

It's all the stuff of great espionage fiction. Yet it happened. The way
the Communist war against Catholicism was conducted, the forms of
ecclesiastical resistance to it that failed, and the resistance strategies that
succeeded all contain important lessons for the future, even as they
clarify the immediate past. That past commands attention and respect
because of the vast human sacrifices it entailed. It also commands
attention for what it can teach about twenty-first-century Catholicism's engagement with new threats to religious freedom.

In a dinner conversation in late 1996, Pope John Paul II's longtime
secretary, Stanisław Dziwisz, said, when speaking of the Catholic
Church's struggle against Communism in Poland, "You must understand that it was *always* 'them' and 'us'." That is, the struggle between
Communism and Catholicism was not a matter of episodic confron-
tations, nor could it be understood by analogy to a parliamentary
government and its opposition. It was all war, all the time.

That was certainly the Communist view of the matter. From the
beginnings of the Bolshevik Revolution, the leaders of Soviet Communism regarded the Catholic Church as a mortal threat to their program and their interests. To Lenin and his successors (including Yuri
Andropov, the only KGB chairman to become leader of the USSR),
the Catholic Church was a vast, wealthy, unscrupulous international
conspiracy whose aims included the demise of Communism and the

destruction of the workers' state. In the post–World War II period, when the United States was known in KGB circles as the "Main Adversary", the Catholic Church was understood to be a formidable ideological adversary. Its influence was feared for what it could do to the Soviet position in various countries of the Warsaw Pact. Its historic cultural links to nationalist sentiment in Lithuania and Ukraine threatened Stalin's inner empire. And it was known to be a principal obstacle to Soviet global objectives, including the export of Marxist-Leninist revolution to the Third World, especially Latin America.

The Communist war against Catholicism intensified exponentially in the last years of World War II as the NKVD (predecessor of the KGB) sought to change the mentality of the populations of the Central and Eastern European countries that were being brought into the Soviet orbit via the bayonets and tanks of the Red Army. It was in these years, for example, that the black legend of Pius XII's alleged indifference to the fate of European Jewry and his alleged sympathies for German National Socialism was manufactured and disseminated by the Soviet intelligence service. Destroying the reputation of the Pope and the Church was thought useful in preparing the ground for the creation of *Homo Sovieticus* east of the Elbe River.

In this season of brutality, clergy and consecrated religious men and women throughout the new Soviet outer empire were subjected to harassment, imprisonment, and death, mere months after being liberated from their Nazi torturers. Some of the surviving resistance heroes of the first decade of the Communist assault on religious liberty are reasonably well known: the Polish primate Stefan Wyszyński, who led that intensely Catholic country's vigorous resistance to Communist attempts to make the Church a subsidiary of the Polish United Workers Party; Hungarian primate Jozef Mindszenty, the living symbol of his people's crushed hopes after Soviet tanks ground down the 1956 Hungarian Revolution; Czech primate Josef Beran, who survived three Nazi concentration camps only to be imprisoned by the Czechoslovak Communist regime; the Croatian leader of Yugoslav Catholicism, Alojzije Stepinac, who, like Mindszenty, endured a classic show trial and who was eventually martyred; the Slovak Jesuit Ján Chryzostom Korec, clandestinely consecrated a bishop in 1951 at the age of twenty-seven, who spent three decades conducting an underground ministry that frequently landed him in labor camps.

The most brutal Communist campaign against the Catholic Church in the immediate postwar period is not so well known, however.

It involved the Greek Catholic Church of Ukraine, Byzantine in its liturgy and polity but in full communion with the Bishop of Rome. Feared by Stalin as the repository of Ukrainian national consciousness and hated by the leadership of Russian Orthodoxy for its adhesion to Rome, the Ukrainian Greek Catholic Church (UGCC) was caught in a political-ecclesiastical vise that snapped shut with lethal force in 1946, when an illegal Sobor, or Church council, was held in L'viv in western Ukraine. Staged by the Soviet secret police with the blessing of Russian Orthodoxy's Moscow patriarchate, the L'viv Sobor dissolved the 1596 Union of Brest, which had brought UGCC into full communion with Rome, and announced that this local church had been "reunited" with Russian Orthodoxy. In one stroke, four million Ukrainian Greek Catholics who declined "reunion" with Russian Orthodoxy became the largest illegal, and underground, religious body in the world. Thousands of Greek Catholics, including numerous priests and all but two of ten Ukrainian Greek Catholic bishops, died in the Gulag.

By the late 1950s, a rough if variegated status quo had been established between the Catholic Church and Communism throughout the Warsaw Pact. The Polish Church was getting stronger under Cardinal Wyszyński's leadership. Hungarian Catholicism was severely weakened by the failed uprising of 1956, while the Church in Czechoslovakia, often functioning underground, was under constant, brutal pressure. The Greek Catholics of Ukraine were worshipping in forests, where they also conducted clandestine schools and seminaries. The Latin-Rite Catholics of Lithuania were holding out against relentless campaigns of both Russification and secularization. It was, as Stanisław Dziwisz said, *always* "'them' and 'us'".

The election of Angelo Roncalli as Pope John XXIII in 1958 marked the beginning of a new phase of this war. Roncalli was concerned that the Church had experienced a certain sclerosis in the latter years of Pius XII. In the first decade of his pontificate, Pius XII had been something of a reformer, encouraging the liturgical movement, giving new impetus to Catholic biblical studies, and trying to get the Church to think of itself in biblical and theological, rather than canonical and legal, categories. If these tentative movements toward reform were to take hold, Roncalli believed, the energies they represented should be focused through an ecumenical council. This papal concern for the renewal of Catholicism's internal life quickly bumped up against the problem of the Communist war against the Church: How were the bishops behind the Iron Curtain to participate in the Second Vatican Council?

This turned out to be less of a problem than anticipated, because the KGB and its sister intelligence services throughout the Warsaw Pact saw Vatican II as a golden opportunity to penetrate the Vatican, deploy new intelligence assets throughout Catholic institutions in Rome, and use the Council's deliberations as a means of strengthening their own grip on restive Catholic populations behind the Iron Curtain. John XXIII's concerns about Central and Eastern European participation at Vatican II, and the new pope's conviction that it was time to test the possibility of a less-frozen relationship between the Holy See and Moscow, combined to give birth to what was known as the Vatican's new Ostpolitik. The Ostpolitik, in turn, seemed even more urgent when the opening of Vatican II coincided with the Cuban Missile Crisis. Where the Pope and the Vatican sought a new dialogue in the interests of world peace, however, the KGB and other Soviet Bloc intelligence agencies sought a new beachhead inside Vatican City in their war against the Catholic Church. The atmosphere of cordial hospitality extended by the Holy See to observers and "separated brethren" at the Council created an ideal situation for this Communist effort to penetrate Catholicism's central administration.

Perhaps the most dramatic Soviet Bloc (SB) attempt to manipulate the work of Vatican II involved an old nemesis, Cardinal Wyszyński of Poland. During its first two working periods, the Council debated how it should discuss the Blessed Virgin Mary—through a separate document or by incorporating a reflection on Mary's role in salvation history into the Dogmatic Constitution on the Church? Colonel Stanisław Morawski, the director of Department IV of the Polish secret intelligence service, charged with anti-Church activities, saw in these theological debates an opportunity to damage Wyszyński's reputation in the world episcopate. So, working with theologians who were SB collaborators, Morawski prepared a memorandum charging Wyszyński with doctrinally dubious views of Mary. The memorandum, "On Selected Aspects of the Cult of the Virgin Mary in Poland", was circulated to all the bishops attending Vatican II, widely distributed in Europe, and regarded as authentic by journalists covering the Council. The Polish primate's standing at Vatican II was at least temporarily weakened.

The manipulation of theological debates for political ends was but one of the methods used by Soviet Bloc intelligence services during Vatican II. From the beginning of the Council's preparatory phase, Polish secret intelligence monitored the work of the Council's preparatory commissions and conducted operations against Polish participants at the Council, including electronic and other forms of surveillance and intensified efforts to recruit collaborators. One well-placed Polish secret police collaborator in Rome, Father Michał Czajkowski (code-named JANKOWSKI), worked with the SB chief at the Polish embassy in Rome and directly with SB Department IV in Warsaw to furnish the secret police and the Polish Communist government with regular reports. The evolution of conciliar texts touching on social and political matters was of obvious interest to Czajkowski's spymasters, but so was the development of ecumenical and interreligious dialogue, in which Communist intelligence services saw new opportunities to create trouble, sow the seeds of division, and weaken local churches.

The Second Vatican Council ran parallel to the first years of the Vatican Ostpolitik, whose principal agent was the Italian curialist and papal diplomat Agostino Casaroli. In his memoirs, Casaroli described the countries of the Warsaw Pact in the early 1960s as a "vast, immobile swamp" that had "finally begun to ripple, though only lightly, under the winds of history". In Casaroli's view (and, one may assume, that of John XXIII and Paul VI), that immobility could not be blamed solely on the animosity of the Kremlin and its satellites; it also reflected the confrontational approach of Pius XII, whose sharp anti-Communist statements allowed the Communist authorities to treat any contacts with the Vatican by citizens of Soviet Bloc countries (including bishops) as acts of espionage. Casaroli also believed that the 1949 Holy Office's Decree against Communism, a decree banning Catholic participation in Communist parties under pain of excommunication, was taken by Communists to be an ongoing "declaration of war".

Casaroli, John XXIII, and Paul VI were also worried about the internal life of the Church behind the Iron Curtain, which, as Casaroli later wrote, was being "suffocated by the coils of a hostile power", such that it would eventually "succumb to a 'natural death'." To prevent this, provision had to be made for the Church's sacramental life: that required priests; ordaining priests required bishops; and getting bishops in place required agreements with Communist governments. So it was thought necessary to find a *modus non moriendi*, as Casaroli put it, a "way of not dying" until such time, perhaps long in the future, when the Cold War would dissolve as a liberalizing Soviet Bloc met an increasingly social-democratic West.

From the Communist point of view, however, the Ostpolitik and the general atmosphere of Vatican openness during the Council provided welcome opportunities to penetrate the Holy See while continuing the work of disintegrating the Catholic Church inside the Warsaw Pact. Thus then-archbishop Casaroli's initial agreement with the Kadar government in Hungary was used by that regime to take control of the Catholic Church in Hungary. Most bishops nominated under the 1964 Vatican-Hungarian agreement cooperated with Hungary's internal security and foreign intelligence services; by 1969, the Hungarian bishops' conference was in large measure controlled by the Hungarian state (which of course meant the Hungarian Communist Party)—so was the Pontifical Hungarian Institute in Rome, all of whose rectors in the late 1960s and half of whose students were trained agents of Hungarian secret intelligence. Roman collaborators who informed their masters in Budapest of Vatican negotiating positions from 1963 on put Vatican diplomats in very disadvantageous positions in their ongoing work with the Kadar regime. The most accomplished of these moles, Fritz Kuzen (MOZART), was an employee of Vatican Radio; MOZART helped prepare Hungarian negotiators for years, not least those involved in the negotiations to end Cardinal Mindszenty's internal exile in the American embassy in Budapest.

Even as the Ostpolitik's early years ran parallel to intensified Soviet persecution of independent elements within the Russian Orthodox Church (ROC), the Soviet government concurrently gave permission for the ROC to be officially represented at the World Council of Churches in Geneva—another opportunity, as the KGB saw it, for disseminating disinformation and propaganda while deploying agents of influence to blunt criticism of the repression of religious freedom behind the Iron Curtain. Later in the 1960s, the Ostpolitik succeeded in gaining permission for a few Lithuanian Catholics to study in Rome. Two Lithuanian KGB agents, ANTANAS and VID-MANTAS, studied at the Gregorian University, while two others, DAKTARAS and ZHIBUTE, participated in meetings of the Vatican commission charged with the reform of canon law.

In 1969, KGB chairman Andropov authorized a new series of active measures against the Vatican, aimed at convincing the Holy See to cease its "subversive activity". KGB assets in the ROC with good Vatican contacts, including the agents DROZDOV (the future patriarch Aleksi II) and ADAMANT (Metropolitan Nikodim, who would die in the arms of Pope John Paul I in 1978), were instructed to "cause dissension between Vatican organizations such as the Congregations for the Eastern Church[es], the Secretariat for Christian Unity, and the Commission for Justice and Peace". ADAMANT was also ordered to warn his curial contacts that he feared the Soviet government would establish autonomous Catholic churches, "independent" of Rome, throughout the USSR. During this same period, the KGB intensified its efforts to destroy the underground Ukrainian Greek Catholic Church, charging one of its leaders, Volodomyr Sterniuk, with sexual improprieties; those charges were also leaked to the Vatican.

All war, all the time, indeed.

Prior to his election as pope, Karol Wojtyła was the object of intense scrutiny by both the Polish SB and the Soviet KGB. Like every other seminarian and priest in postwar Poland, Wojtyła had an SB file and an SB watcher from the outset of his ecclesiastical life; the file thickened and the number of watchers intensified after Wojtyła's consecration in 1958 as auxiliary bishop of Kraków. During the next twenty years, the SB came to loathe and fear Wojtyła even more than they feared Cardinal Wyszyński. It was not a question of Wyszyński losing his edge; rather, the dance between Wyszyński and the regime was one with which both sides were familiar. With Wojtyła, the regime never knew what might happen. And as the archbishop of

Kraków found his voice as a defender of the human rights of all, he came to be seen as an even greater threat than Wyszyński.

In November 1973, the SB's Department IV created "Independent Group D", which was assigned the task of "distintegrating" Polish Catholicism through a coordinated attack on the Church's integrity. The leader of Independent Group D, SB colonel Konrad Straszewski, had been the secret-police contact of one of Wojtyła's colleagues at the Catholic University of Lublin, Father Mieczysław Krąpiec, O.P., for years. The reports on Wojtyła from Straszewski and other SB agents led Polish prosecutors to consider charging the archbishop of Kraków with sedition on three occasions in 1973–1974. Things had changed since the heyday of Polish Stalinism, however, and Communist leader Edward Gierek did not dare do to Wojtyła what his predecessors had done to Wyszyński in 1953. So the surveillance of the archbishop increased, as did the efforts to suborn his associates in the archdiocesan chancery. And then there was the brutality: Monsignor Andrzej Bardecki, ecclesiastical advisor to the lay-run Catholic newspaper *Tygodnik Powszechny,* was beaten senseless by SB (or SB-inspired) thugs one night after leaving an editorial meeting that Cardinal Wojtyła also attended. Visiting the elderly priest in the hospital the next day, the archbishop said, "You replaced me; you were beaten instead of me." (Interestingly enough, the SB never attempted to suborn Wojtyła's close lay friends, thus exhibiting a peculiar Communist form of clericalism.)

The SB did not discover the clandestine ordinations of priests for underground service in Czechoslovakia that Cardinal Wojtyła conducted in Kraków. But the secret police did know about, and could not have been pleased by, the archbishop's increasingly close contacts with lay (and often agnostic) Polish political dissidents in the mid-1970s. At a 1975 KGB-organized conference of Soviet Bloc intelligence agencies, summoned to plan further anti-Vatican activities, the Polish, Hungarian, and Czechoslovak secret services all reported "significant agent positions" in the Vatican, while the Hungarians warned that Wojtyła would be an especially dangerous opponent as pope.

Yuri Andropov evidently agreed. Shortly after the election of Pope John Paul II on October 16, 1978, the KGB sent several clandestine agents, known in the trade as "illegals", into Poland to gather what intelligence they could. One of them, Oleg Petrovich Buryen (DEREVLYOV), posed as the representative of a Canadian publishing company interested in Polish missionaries in Asia and made an assiduous effort to cultivate the new pope's old friend and fellow philosopher Father Józef Tischner. The Polish SB, for its part, marked their countryman's election as Bishop of Rome by deploying to the Eternal City a particularly sophisticated agent, Edward Kotowski (PIETRO), who, for the previous three years, had been given intense Italian-language training and told to learn everything he could about the Holy See and its ways. Working clandestinely under the cover of a diplomatic posting at the Polish embassy in Rome, PIETRO cultivated an extensive network of Vatican contacts, including men who had at least some access to the papal apartment. PIETRO later told Polish historian Andrzej Grajewski that, during the early years of John Paul II's pontificate, more than half of the "diplomats" working at the Polish embassy in Rome were in fact working for the SB, as were Rome-based employees of the Polish state airline and travel agency, members of the Polish trade mission to Italy, and various "illegals".

John Paul II suspected that the Holy See had been penetrated by Soviet Bloc intelligence and changed the papal routine to provide some measure of counterintelligence capacity. Materials dealing with Poland and other sensitive matters were no longer archived for ready reference in the Vatican's Secretariat of State; rather, they were kept in the papal apartment, where there was no chance for mischief-makers to prowl about. John Paul also declined to dictate memoranda of conversations with notables such as Soviet foreign minister Andrei Gromyko, evidently concerned that such notes might fall into the wrong hands somewhere along the curial paper trail. So he and his secretary, Stanisław Dziwisz, got together every night to review the day's appointments and conversations, Dziwisz keeping notes in a series of diaries that remained under his control in the papal apartment.

Of particular interest throughout Soviet Bloc intelligence was the proposed papal visit to Poland in June 1979. Prior to the visit, the Polish SB mounted an enormous damage-limitation operation, LATO-79 (Summer-79), which managed to insert at least one clerical mole into the Church's planning commission for the papal visit. On this occasion, the SB worked in close collaboration with the East German intelligence service, the Stasi, whose legendary spymaster, Markus Wolf, had his own asset in the Vatican: a German Benedictine, Eugen Brammertz (LICHTBLICK), who worked for the German edition of *L'Osservatore Romano*. While the Pope was in Poland, igniting a revolution of conscience that quickly spread throughout the region, the SB deployed 480 agents in Kraków alone to monitor events and cause what trouble they could.

The intensity of concern displayed by the SB and the Stasi before and during the June 1979 papal pilgrimage was matched in Moscow, where the KGB charged the Polish pope with "ideological subversion". Moscow was particularly upset that John Paul had referred to himself as a "Slav pope"; this led the Soviet Communist Party's Politburo to conclude, in what would have been a surprise to Vatican diplomats, that the Holy See had launched a new "ideological struggle against the socialist countries". Five months later, the Central Committee secretariat of the Soviet Communist Party approved a six-point plan entitled "Decision to Work Against the Policies of the Vatican in Relation with Socialist States", which included an active-measures campaign in the West to "demonstrate that the leadership of the new pope, John Paul II, is dangerous to the Catholic Church". In this context, "active measures" meant propaganda, disinformation campaigns, blackmail, and an attempt to persuade the world press that the Pope was a threat to peace. Soviet fears intensified by an order of magnitude the following year with the rise of the Solidarity movement, an enterprise that Yuri Andropov immediately sought to influence through the infiltration of more "illegals" into Poland. The Pope's warning against an anti-Solidarity Soviet invasion of Poland in December 1980, conveyed in a personal letter to Soviet president Leonid Brezhnev, added yet another item to the bill of indictment that eventually was served on John Paul by Mehmet Ali Agca on May 13, 1981.

The failed assassination attempt was not the end of the Communist war against John Paul II, however. That war took a nasty turn during the difficult negotiations preceding the second papal pilgrimage to Poland in June 1983, when the country was still under martial law. Eager to gain the upper hand, the SB decided to blackmail John Paul. The instrument chosen was a fake diary, said to have been written by a deceased former employee of the archdiocese of Kraków during Wojtyła's archbishopric, in which the "diarist", Irina Kinaszewska, reported that she had been the archbishop's lover. The plot unraveled when Grzegorz Piotrowski of Independent Group D, the man charged with planting the fake diary in the home of Monsignor Bardecki, got roaring drunk after the successful break-in, crashed his car, and told the traffic police what he had been up to. Word of the plot began to leak out of police circles, as it did from the Kraków chancery when the fake diary was discovered and recognized for what it was. Thus the plot to blackmail the Pope self-destructed.

The diary affair has something of the feel of the incompetent Keystone Kops of the silent film comedies—until one recognizes just how deeply the SB (and the Polish government) feared John Paul II, even in a country under martial law, and how low they were prepared to sink in order to undermine his moral authority. As for Captain Piotrowski, he would reappear a year and a half later: as the man who beat Father Jerzy Popiełuszko to death and dumped his battered body into the Vistula River.

All war, all the time.

It will be decades, perhaps centuries, before the full story of the Communist war against the Catholic Church is told. Yet given the new availability of materials from Communist governmental and secret-police archives, some lessons from this struggle can be drawn. The first involves the nature of the conflict and the limits of dialogue.

Catholicism and Communism offered the world two radically different visions of human nature, human community, human origins, and human destiny. These visions were fundamentally incompatible, which explains in part the ferocity of the animus Communism directed against the Church. That incompatibility also suggests that the strategic vision of John Paul II, which encompassed the victory of freedom over totalitarian tyranny, was more acute than those who imagined a slow convergence between liberalizing Communism and an increasingly social-democratic West. There would be no convergence here. Someone was going to win, and someone was going to lose. As it happened, the truth about the human person proved its strength over time. The sacrifice of the martyrs reminds us that that proving involved severe testing and great heroism.

This truth about the nature of the conflict bears reflection when considering the threats to religious freedom and other basic human rights posed by China, Vietnam, North Korea, and Cuba, and by jihadist Islamism (which, in power, takes on many of the characteristics of Western totalitarianism). What lessons might be drawn from the experience of the Vatican Ostpolitik in the 1960s and 1970s for the Church's relations with China, Vietnam, and Cuba today? What lessons might be drawn from that experience for the Church's struggle to survive in the Arab Islamic world? And, to press the question into territory where Western political leaders do not want to go, does the Church's experience vis-à-vis Communism offer lessons about the twenty-first-century Church's relationship to aggressive, exclusivist secularism and its attempts to impose on Western democracies what Cardinal Joseph Ratzinger called in April 2005 a "dictatorship of relativism"?

In reflecting on those questions, it should be recognized that the Catholic attempt to find a modus vivendi (or, in Cardinal Casaroli's term, *modus non moriendi*) with Communist powers rarely, if ever, paid significant dividends. In fact, the problem of the Church's relationship with political systems that attempt to fill all space in society long antedates the rise of Russian Bolshevism. Appeasement did not work with Napoleon; it did not work with Mexican or Spanish anticlerical regimes; it did not work in post-Anschluss Austria; so it should not have been a surprise that it did not work with Communism.

The most poignant of the Ostpolitik's failures was in Hungary, where the Church's integrity was gravely compromised by the post-Mindszenty episcopal leadership and its acquiescence to the Hungarian Communist regime; the effects of that failure are still felt today. The countercase to Hungary was Poland, where history will judge Cardinal Wyszyński a better strategist and tactician than the architects of the Vatican Ostpolitik. Stubborn, courageous, and unapologetic resistance kept Catholicism alive in Lithuania and Ukraine; acquiescence and appeasement were destroying the Church in Bohemia and Moravia until John Paul II inspired the octogenarian Cardinal František Tomášek to become a resistance hero in the 1980s.

Successful resistance, in turn, was based on a strong sense of Catholic identity, coupled with the kind of political shrewdness displayed by Stefan Wyszyński and Karol Wojtyła, a shrewdness that combined steadiness of strategic vision with tactical flexibility. Wyszyński's attempts to find space for the Polish Church to recover its strength after World War II were not always appreciated by the Vatican of the late 1940s, where the strategic goal (that Communism must be defeated) was clear, but the tactical circumstances in Poland were not so well understood. The situation was reversed in the 1970s, with the Vatican urging tactical flexibility (aimed at establishing formal diplomatic relations between the Holy See and the Polish People's Republic) while Wyszyński took a tactical hard line, correctly fearing Communist efforts to play "divide and conquer", with the diplomats of the Holy See as unwitting pawns on the chessboard.

For his part, Karol Wojtyła, Pope John Paul II, was shrewd enough to understand that appointing the architect of Paul VI's Ostpolitik, Agostino Casaroli, as his own secretary of state created tactical advantages for the Church. As the Pope preached moral revolution over the heads of Communist regimes, speaking directly to their people, Casaroli continued his diplomacy, thus denying the Communists the opportunity to charge that the Church had reneged on its commitment to dialogue. It cannot be said that Cardinal Casaroli's memoirs reveal any great appreciation for this division of labor. In fact, Casaroli's 1990 praise of Mikhail Gorbachev as the pivotal figure in the Revolution of 1989 (in a lecture in Kraków, no less) suggests that this ablest of Vatican diplomats never really grasped the full genius of John Paul II's approach. Still, John Paul and Casaroli made a formidable team, if not precisely in the way Casaroli (who once said, wistfully, that "I would like to help this pope, but I find him so different") would have wanted.

The Catholic Church's experience with Soviet Communism may also hold lessons for the Church's relationship with Russian Orthodoxy and the Russian state today. Russian Orthodoxy counts many thousands of noble martyrs among its twentieth-century gifts to God. Yet from the end of the Second World War through the collapse of the USSR, the Russian Orthodox leadership was largely a subsidiary of the KGB. The 1974 Furov Report by the Soviet Council on Religious Affairs distinguished three categories of Russian Orthodox bishops; the first category included those "who affirm in word and deed not only loyalty but patriotism toward the socialist society; strictly observe the laws on cults, and educate the parish clergy and believers in the same spirit; realistically understand that our state is not interested in proclaiming the role of religion and the Church in society; and, realizing this, do not display any particular activeness in extending the influence of Orthodoxy among the population". The bishops in this category included Patriarch Pimen, who refused to invite John Paul II to Moscow for the 1988 celebration of the millennium of Christianity among the eastern Slavs, and Patriarch Aleksi II, the successor to Pimen who refused to allow John Paul II to come to post-Communist Russia.

Patriarch Pimen's praise for the "lofty spiritual qualities" of Yuri Andropov, chief persecutor of Soviet Christians for decades, is an example at the outer boundaries of toadying to power. But praise for the czar of the day is not an anomaly in Russian Orthodoxy history. That pattern of collaboration continues today with the current patriarch, Kirill, whose support for the revanchism of Vladimir Putin has put a considerable strain on relations between the ROC, on the one hand, and the Ukrainian Greek Catholic and Ukrainian Orthodox communities in Ukraine, on the other. Kirill's appointment as an ROC representative to the World Council of Churches in Geneva when he was a twenty-five-year-old newly ordained priest could not have been anything other than the work of the KGB. It might have been hoped that this intelligent, sophisticated man had disengaged himself from his previous political entanglements by the time of his election as patriarch, which was eight years after the Soviet Union imploded. But the first decade of his patriarchate, during which he insisted on certain territories being the exclusive cultural sphere of Russian Orthodoxy, was not reassuring, as Kirill's statements on the "Russian world" closely mirrored those of Vladimir Putin. Thus the time would seem to have come for the Catholic-Russian Orthodox dialogue to focus on certain basic questions of church-state relations. Proposals by the Moscow patriarchate for a joint Catholic-Russian Orthodox "new evangelization" in Europe will lie fallow until a mutual baseline of understanding about the proper relationship of Christian churches to state authority, and about the nonethnically determined character of the free act of faith, has been established.

Finally, the ferocity of the Communist assault on the Church, in which Christians were fed to wild animals and crucified for the first time since the days of Diocletian, offers an important lesson about ultramundane politics wedded to modern technology in societies devoid of transcendent moral reference points that provide a cultural check on state power. The slaughters of the European wars of religion took place almost four centuries ago; the far greater slaughters of twentieth-century Communism took place within living memory. That historical fact might usefully be raised in Brussels, Washington, and various European capitals when alarms are sounded about the alleged dangers of religiously informed moral argument in the public square.

The Communist war against Christianity was a bloody affair, in which Christian martyrdom reached new heights of sacrifice. That war also involved billions of man-hours of work and billions of dollars of public expenditure and was thus a form of theft from civil society. Deeply committed and politically shrewd Christian pastors and laity eventually won out over Communism. The blood of martyrs, however, was the seed of the Church's victory. Their sacrifice and what can be learned from it about the cardinal virtue of fortitude (courage) must never be forgotten.

# Grand Strategy Reconsidered

## *The Statecraft of a Saint*

When the Catholic Church celebrated the canonizations of Pope John Paul II and Pope John XXIII on April 27, 2014, the Church was not "making saints", and neither was Pope Francis. Rather, the Church and the Pope were recognizing two saints that God had made, publicly declaring its conviction that, in these two men of our time, the grace conferred in baptism had borne fruit in a heroic exercise of the theological virtues of faith, hope, and love, and the cardinal virtues of prudence, justice, courage, and moderation. In canonizing John Paul II, then, the Catholic Church was not recommending the Polish pope as an exemplar of shrewd and effective statecraft, as scholars and political leaders might lift up Benjamin Disraeli or Dean Acheson as models of statesmanship. Still, John Paul II's heroic exercise of the chief virtue of statecraft (prudence) contains important lessons for those practicing the arts of governance on a global stage in the twenty-first century.

Pope John Paul II always insisted, correctly, that he was neither diplomat nor politician. He was, rather, a pastor who in exercising his pastoral responsibilities had things to say to the world of political power, because those things had to do with the Church's defense of human dignity, the protection of which gives the exercise of public authority a distinctive excellence and a fundamental moral purpose. Yet this Polish-born pastor who refused to don the mantle of politician or diplomat, choosing instead the role of moral witness, was the most politically consequential pope in centuries, a pope whose evangelically inspired action changed history and left a deep impression on the future. The footprints of his distinctive statecraft can be found all over the world: in Central and Eastern Europe, which he helped liberate from Communism; in Latin America, Asia, and Africa, where

men and women formed by John Paul II's social doctrine are striving
to make freedom for excellence work in the political and economic
fields; in the United States, Canada, and Western Europe, where
John Paul II's robust defense of religious freedom as the first of human
rights has taken on new salience in postmodern societies threatened
by an aggressive secularism that regards religious conviction as merely
a personal lifestyle choice and that seeks to drive communities formed
by such convictions out of public life.

To be sure, the responsibilities of a pope and the responsibilities
of presidents, prime ministers, members of legislatures, diplomats,
and other public officials are not identical. Popes no longer deploy
hard power in the form of armies, as they once did; democratic
leaders charged with the defense of the common good must cal-
culate the interests of the people they represent and serve in ways
that popes don't—which is to say that popes and public officials
deal with international politics out of different tool kits. Still, at a
historical moment in which statecraft is sometimes misunderstood
as a form of psychotherapy, the post–Cold War order seems to be
coming unhinged, and the West is unsure of itself and its role as the
guarantor of a measure of decency and stability in world affairs, it's
useful to reflect on what we can learn from the distinctive global
statecraft of a saint who had a real impact on what the pundits are
pleased to call the "real world".


## The First Lesson: Culture Drives History

John Paul II's statecraft rejected the fallacies that made political
modernity a slaughterhouse. He rejected the Jacobin fallacy, born
in 1789, that history is driven by politics, understood as the quest
for power, understood as my ability to impose my will on you. He
rejected the Marxist fallacy that "history" is merely the exhaust fumes
of the means of production. And he rejected the liberal fallacy that
if a society only gets the machinery of democracy and the free economy right, those machines can run by themselves. Rather, drawing
on both Catholic and Polish sources, John Paul II insisted that culture was, is, and always will be the most dynamic force in history,
allowing us to resist tyranny and inspiring us to build and sustain free

societies. Moreover, he understood that at the center of culture is cult, or religion: what people believe, cherish, and worship; what people are willing to stake their lives, and their children's lives, on.

This culture-first approach to history and statecraft was on full display during John Paul's first papal pilgrimage to Poland, nine days in June 1979 on which the history of the twentieth century pivoted. The Nine Days are often described as a moment of national catharsis, and there is undoubtedly something to that: the pent-up frustrations, sorrows, and angers engendered by Poland's awful experiences over two centuries—its vivisection in the late nineteenth century, its demolition by Nazis, and its desecration by Communists—began to be healed by the triumphant return to his homeland of Poland's papal son. But a lot more was happening in Poland in June 1979 than catharsis. The papal visit empowered a profound *transformation*: the revitalization of culture in a revolution of conscience, which led in turn to the restoration of a vital civil society.

The Nine Days of John Paul II in June 1979 were, arguably, the most politically potent papal intervention in world affairs since the High Middle Ages. Yet the Pope didn't mention politics or economics *once*. Rather, John Paul spoke the truth about Poland's history, its culture, and its national self-understanding, saying, in dozens of variations on one great theme, "You are not who *they* say you are. Remember who you really are, own the truth of your history and your culture, and you will find tools of resistance that totalitarianism cannot match." By returning to his people the truth about themselves, the Pope gave Poles the raw materials with which to forge tools of liberation that were essentially moral and cultural in nature. Deployed over a hard decade of struggle that led to the triumphs of the Revolution of 1989, those tools proved more than adequate in answering Stalin's cynical question: "The pope? How many divisions does he have?"

## The Second Lesson: Ideas Count, for Good and for Ill

I doubt that John Paul II ever read John Maynard Keynes. But he certainly understood the truth of what the Cambridge economist meant when he wrote that ideas, "both when they are right and when they are wrong, are more powerful than is commonly understood. Indeed the world is ruled by little else. Practical men, who believe themselves to be quite exempt from any intellectual influences, are usually the slaves of some defunct economist. Madmen in authority, who hear voices in the air, are distilling their frenzy from some academic scribbler of a few years back.... Soon or late, it is ideas ... which are dangerous for good or evil."

Karol Wojtyła knew the danger in false ideas from hard personal experience. Living in what Timothy Snyder aptly dubbed the "bloodlands" of East Central Europe, he had seen the lethal effects of Lenin's, Stalin's, and Hitler's wicked ideas in the deaths of tens of millions of human beings, including his friends and classmates. But he also knew from experience the regenerative power of noble ideas—for example, the ideas of Christian Democracy deployed by men like Konrad Adenauer, Alcide de Gasperi, and Robert Schuman in rebuilding postwar Europe and laying the foundations for the continent's twenty-first-century peace and prosperity. In both cases—the wicked, false, and death-dealing ideas, and the good, true, and ennobling ideas—what was most crucial, in John Paul II's view, was the idea of the human person being proposed. Or to use a social science term in its philosophical sense, what counted was *anthropology*.

And here we find the connection between Karol Wojtyła, Polish philosopher, and John Paul II, statesman. In the first decade of his pontificate, John Paul II, statesman, saw that the Yalta division of Europe was not only wrong but fragile and unsustainable, because Karol Wojtyła, Polish philosopher, knew that Stalin's power grab in the waning days of the Second World War was in service to a false idea of the human person, a warped anthropology that led inevitably to the Gulag, the KGB, the Berlin Wall, and the rest of the apparatus of Soviet repression. In the last years of his papacy, John Paul II, statesman, knew that twenty-first-century Europe risked dissolving into incoherence because Karol Wojtyła, Polish philosopher, had accurately measured the deficiencies of the atheistic humanism and soul-withering secularism that were at the root of Europe's post–Cold War crisis of civilizational morale.

Thus, practitioners of statecraft who wish to learn from the example of John Paul II will take ideas, and the war of ideas, with as much seriousness as indices of gross national product or measures of military capability. Why? Because all three are connected. Neither wealth nor military power can be usefully deployed in the cause of freedom if the will to do so is not present. And it seems unlikely that the West will form such a will—the will to challenge the lies and propaganda of the forces of disorder as a precondition to restoring a measure of order to world affairs—if our culture continues to be eroded from within by skepticism and relativism, by an anthropology that reduces the human person to a mere bundle of desires, and by a nihilism that mocks all religious and moral conviction.

## The Third Lesson: Don't Psychologize the Adversary

One result of the decline of political philosophy and the concurrent rise of social science in the late modern and postmodern West has been the emergence of psychological approaches to statecraft. In America one can trace this back to the social science theories popular among the "best and brightest" of the Kennedy/Johnson years: the mandarins who believed that a naval blockade of Cuba in 1962 was a form of "communication" and who imagined that "signaling" North Vietnam by turning the spigot of air power on and off could change Ho Chi Minh's behavior. The Obama-era analogues to this psychologization of statecraft were the notorious "resets", first with Russia and the Arab Islamic world, then with Cuba, then with Iran. The premise here is that bad guys behave badly because of what *we* do, so that if we behave differently, *their* behavior will change and become less disagreeable, if not downright praiseworthy.

John Paul II knew this for the foolishness it was and is. As a keen student of the human condition, he understood that bad guys behave badly because of who they are, what they espouse, and what they seek, not because of anything "we" did to "them". Thus he could focus on the issues at hand—for example, religious freedom and other basic human rights in the Communist world—without paralyzing himself in spasms of self-flagellation because the Cold War division of Europe was somehow Harry Truman's fault. Unlike Western revisionist historians, John Paul understood that Stalin, his heirs, and their Polish epigones did what they did because of who they were and what they sought, not because good old Uncle Joe had been offended by the haberdasher from Independence, Missouri, at the Potsdam Conference in July 1945.

The twenty-first-century lessons to be drawn should be obvious. To take one urgent case: Vladimir Putin is doing what he's doing in Ukraine, Moldova, the Baltic states, and elsewhere, not because of anything Ukraine, Moldova, or other post-Soviet states did to him or to Russia, but because of who he is, what he believes, and what he seeks. Thus accounts of the war Putin launched in Ukraine that seek to "balance" responsibilities for the conflict (or, worse, describe it as a "civil war") distort reality and in doing so make creative and sensible policy virtually impossible. The same is true of the clerical totalitarians who hold ultimate authority in Tehran. Unless their behavior in seeking a nuclear capability is understood on its own terms as an expression of their apocalyptic ideas and ambitions rather than as a reaction to pressures from the Sunni world, the West, or both, the world will remain vulnerable to Iranian dissembling and stalling, and the likelihood of an Iranian bomb will grow accordingly.

### The Fourth Lesson: Speak Clearly, and Occasionally Loudly, and Be Supple in Deploying Whatever Large or Small Sticks You Have at Hand

When John Paul II was elected the 264th Bishop of Rome on October 16, 1978, Vatican diplomacy was well into the second decade of its Ostpolitik, an approach to the problems of local Catholic churches behind the Iron Curtain that avoided public condemnation of Communism's human rights violations for the sake of reaching diplomatic agreements with Warsaw Pact countries. Those agreements were supposed to guarantee the Church's freedom to live its sacramental life by its own standards. In the event, however, what limited agreements were achieved demoralized the Resistance Church in several Eastern Bloc countries, turned the Catholic Church in Hungary into a subsidiary of the Hungarian party-state, did nothing to relieve the condition of Catholics in the Soviet Union, and opened the Vatican to further penetration by Communist intelligence services, a process that had begun in the early 1960s.

Yet John Paul was shrewd enough not to dismantle the Ostpolitik of Pope Paul VI and his principal diplomat, Archbishop Agostino

Casaroli. Rather, he made Casaroli his own secretary of state, named him a cardinal, and gave him free rein to pursue his diplomacy east of the Elbe River. Thus no Communist leader could publicly accuse the Church of reneging on her previous commitments because of a "reactionary" Polish pope in league with NATO. (Of course, Soviet and Eastern Bloc propaganda and disinformation campaigns worked overtime to sell precisely that message throughout the West, not without some success.) But while Casaroli continued his bilateral diplomatic efforts, John Paul II restored clarity to, and raised the volume of, the Catholic Church's voice, challenging human rights violations and calling upon Communist states to honor their human rights commitments under Basket Three of the 1975 Helsinki Final Act— and did so by making his own voice the Vatican's principal voice. Time and again, in venue after venue, John Paul II lifted up the first freedom, religious freedom, and brought his case before the world in his 1979 address to the U.N. General Assembly. And because of that papal megaphone (and its amplification by Radio Free Europe and Radio Liberty), the Church resistance behind the Iron Curtain knew it had a champion; those in the West who were working to support the Resistance Church in Central and Eastern Europe were inspired to expand their efforts; and all the while, the Soviet rationale for the Cold War was being systematically undermined in the order of ideas.

The Polish pope applied the same methods to shore up Catholic leaders working for justice and peace in Central America in the face of Marxist governments and insurgencies there. The Sandinista tide began to recede when John Paul II vocally confronted the adolescent cheerleading of Daniel Ortega and his comrades at a 1983 papal Mass in Managua. (Thanks to some adroit work by the papal trip planner, Father Roberto Tucci, S.J., the entire affair, including the Pope demanding "*Silencio!*" from Ortega & Co. so that he could preach his sermon, was telecast throughout the region.) Yet John Paul was also willing to be the quiet persuader, working behind the scenes while local churchmen did the denouncing of injustice, when that seemed appropriate. This method worked well in Argentina, Chile, and the Philippines, where the Pope met with (and thus endorsed and gave protection to) local human rights activists and political reformers while he worked privately on the Argentine military, on General Augusto Pinochet, and on President Ferdinand Marcos, urging them to respect human rights and restore democracy in their countries.

The lesson for the twenty-first-century statesman: moral pressure can be an important lever in world politics, but effective human rights advocacy and democracy promotion require dexterity—diplomatic dexterity, and dexterity in waging the battle of ideas.

## The Fifth Lesson: Listen to the Martyrs

The Ostpolitik that dominated Vatican diplomacy for the fifteen years prior to the election of John Paul II did not dishonor the persecuted local churches behind the Iron Curtain. But it did tend to regard their intransigence as an obstacle to diplomatic accommodations between the Holy See and Communist regimes. And such accommodations had to be reached, according to the Ostpolitik, because the Yalta division of Europe was a permanent reality of world politics, not a temporary aberration. Thus in the decade prior to John Paul's election, Pope Paul VI removed Cardinals Josef Beran and József Mindszenty from their posts in Prague and Budapest and kept the exiled leader of the Greek Catholic Church in Soviet-occupied Ukraine, Cardinal Josyf Slipyj, at a distance.

John Paul II had long viewed the witness of the martyr-confessors in the underground churches behind the Iron Curtain differently. To his mind, the witness of these brave men and women, living and dead, helped strengthen a religiously informed cultural resistance to Communism because it uniquely embodied the moral pressure that could and should be exerted on Communist regimes. So during his time as archbishop of Kraków, Wojtyła clandestinely ordained priests for service in the underground Church in Czechoslovakia, in what amounted to a tacit challenge to the Vatican's Ostpolitik. As pope, he made sure that the world (and especially the Kremlin) knew of his meeting with the Ukrainian cardinal Slipyj, a longtime Gulag prisoner and leader of the world's largest underground Church, a month after his election. That meeting took place a few weeks after he had sent his own cardinal's zucchetto to the Ostrabrama shrine at Vilnius in Lithuania as a gesture of solidarity with another long-suffering and bitterly persecuted local Church, a gesture that was repaid within weeks as the Lithuanian Committee for the Defense of Believers' Rights was formed and became one of the most dogged human rights proponents in the Soviet Union.

This pattern continued throughout the pontificate and was not limited to the Pope's support for fellow Catholics. John Paul II used personal contacts familiar with life and current events in the USSR to keep himself informed of the views of the hard-pressed human rights resistance there. One result: his December 1985 meeting in the Vatican with Elena Bonner, wife of Andrei Sakharov, which was arranged by one of John Paul's informal agents, Irina Ilovayskaya Alberti, former aide to Aleksandr Solzhenitsyn in his Vermont exile.

For John Paul II, the witness of the modern martyr-confessors deserved honor and respect in its own right. Just as the Church demeaned itself, he believed, when it accommodated the demands of totalitarian persecutors, so the Church was strengthened by acknowledging the witness of its sons and daughters who had taken the risk of freedom and paid the price for it. Honoring the persecuted Church also had an important effect on the Holy See's diplomatic action in world politics, acting as a brake against the Realpolitik pragmatism that, while common in European foreign ministries, is neither realistic nor pragmatic over the long haul.

There are lessons here for dealing with such twenty-first-century challenges as the transition to a post-Communist future in Cuba and China, and in responding to the lethal threats posed by jihadist Islam to Christian communities in the Middle East and Africa. Listening to the voices of the martyr-confessors of these regions will clarify the true nature of the challenges posed by the Cuban and Chinese regimes and by jihadists, thus erecting another barrier against the psychologization of conflict. Lifting up the witness of the living martyr-confessors publicly and persistently might also afford them a measure of protection, while helping sustain islands of civil society essential to future progress toward justice and peace in Cuba, China, the Middle East, and Africa.

## The Sixth Lesson: Think Long-Term and Do Not Sacrifice Core Principles to What Seems Immediate Advantage

In the mid-1980s, after martial law had been lifted in Poland but while the independent self-governing trade union Solidarity was still legally banned, officials of General Wojciech Jaruzelski's

Communist regime sounded out senior Polish Church leaders with a proposal: the regime would open a national dialogue on Poland's future, and the Church would act as the regime's interlocutor. Some Polish churchmen were tempted by the offer. But John Paul II declined the bait. Solidarity was the proper representative of Polish civil society, in his view, and the Church ought not substitute itself in that role, especially when that meant tacitly acquiescing to Solidarity's legal nonstatus. The Church could help facilitate a conversation between the regime and the opposition, but the Church would not replace the opposition.

That decision had theological roots. In John Paul II's ecclesiology, the Church could not be a partisan political actor, because that role contradicted the eucharistic character of the Church (a theme he stressed in his challenge to various forms of Latin American liberation theology). It also reflected the strategic vision of John Paul II's social doctrine, in which the Church formed the people who formed the civil society and the political institutions that did the work of politics; the Church was not a political agent in its own right, although the Church obviously had a voice in society.

In the event, the Church's refusal to play "opposition party" to the "leading role" of the Communist Party in Poland increased the pressure on the Jaruzelski regime to recognize the real Polish opposition, represented by Solidarity. Thus John Paul II's principled decision helped create the conditions for the possibility of the Polish Round Table of early 1989 and the partially free elections of June 1989. And those elections, by delivering an overwhelming victory to Solidarity, made possible the first non-Communist government in postwar Polish history.

The lesson here, for both twenty-first-century statesmen and the diplomats of the Holy See, seems to be this: the cause of freedom and the cause of the Church are best served when churchmen acting as statesmen think long-term and do not bracket or minimize core principles for what can seem immediate advantage. That lesson bears on the Church's role in Cuba today, where local Catholic leaders' understandable desire to strengthen the Church's institutional infrastructure should go hand in hand with a vigorous defense of the dissidents who form the core of the Cuban civil society of the future. A two-pronged strategy of building while resisting is most likely to midwife a post–Castro future while preparing the ground for the task of reconverting Cuba after its liberation.

This sixth lesson also suggests cautions about the possibility of establishing full diplomatic relations between the Holy See and the People's Republic of China. In the present circumstances, any such deal would require the Vatican to sever its diplomatic exchange with the Republic of China on Taiwan, the first Chinese democracy in history. What signal would such a deal, with such a price tag, send about the Catholic Church's vision of China's future? What signal would it send about the Church's concern for the hard-pressed and often persecuted elements of civil society that exist in China today and are pressing for a nonauthoritarian and open future? The evangelical mission of the Church in the mainland China of the future is not going to be materially advanced by accommodating the Chinese Communist regime too easily.

There are also lessons here for the Holy See's role in Ukraine. The Vatican's long-standing preoccupation with maintaining cordial ecumenical relations and serious theological dialogue with the Russian Orthodox Church should be reassessed in light of the fact that, in the Ukrainian drama that began with the 2013–2014 Maidan Revolution of Dignity, the Russian Orthodox leadership has functioned as an agent of Russian state power, playing its own sorry role in the Kremlin's propaganda and disinformation campaigns. Neither common ecumenical witness in defense of international legal norms nor serious theological dialogue is possible under these circumstances. Pretending otherwise merely reinforces the damage being done by aggressors and their clerical allies.

## The Seventh Lesson: Media "Reality" Isn't Necessarily Reality

The most unintentionally hilarious commentary on the public impact of Pope John Paul II came from the editorial page of the *New York Times*. John Paul was in the middle of those epic nine days of June 1979 when, on June 5, the *Times* ran an editorial on the papal pilgrimage with this conclusion: "As much as the visit of Pope John Paul II to Poland must reinvigorate and reinspire the Roman

Catholic Church in Poland, it does not threaten the political order of the nation or of Eastern Europe."

Well, not quite.

Why did the *Times* so badly miss the reality of what was afoot in Poland? In part, I suspect, because it regarded "the Roman Catholic Church in Poland" as of no more political consequence to "the political order of the nation or of Eastern Europe" than the Polish Flat-Earth Society (which, come to think of it, is not a bad analogue for the *Times'* general view of the Catholic Church). Then there was the view in the American liberal world (for which the *Times* was both mirror and infallible teaching authority) that the Cold War would be resolved when an increasingly social democratic West "converged" with a liberalizing East and the Berlin Wall would simply dissolve—a "narrative" also popular in certain Western European (and indeed Vatican) circles. And then there was the *Times'* concern, shared by many foreign policy "realists" in the West, that any disturbance of the Yalta postwar order threatened nuclear holocaust. So, while it might be too bad for what were once called the "captive nations", the way things were was the way things were going to have to be, lest greater demons be set loose.

These narratives—the narrative of the political irrelevance of religion in the late twentieth century; the narrative of "convergence"; and the change-risks-nuclear-war narrative—seemed to be reality. But they weren't reality. John Paul II was wise enough to know that and to act according to what was really reality: that a morally informed human rights resistance, based on a clear and correct conception of the dignity of the human person, would attack Communism at its most vulnerable point, and thus held one of the keys to settling the Cold War in favor of the forces of freedom.

The problem of confusing reality with "media reality" or narrative has intensified since 1979, in no small part because of the ubiquity of social media and instant Internet commentary, both of which readily create narratives that seem to be reality. Yet the statesmen of the twenty-first century would do well to take a lesson from John Paul II and read the "signs of the times" with their own eyes, rather than through lenses befogged by media-generated narratives. The same lesson applies to churchmen. Church leaders, clerical and lay, who respond to media-generated narratives about the Catholic Church rather than to the imperatives of the Gospel are not going to advance either the evangelical mission of the Church or the cause of human dignity and freedom. The Gospel has power, and its power can cut through the densest of false narratives.

The dramatic life of John Paul II displayed many admirable qualities worth emulating. But in the confused first decades of the twenty-first century, his refusal to submit to the tyranny of the possible is the most compelling and inspiring characteristic of the man.

The great hopes that followed the Revolution of 1989, the collapse of the Soviet Union, the various color revolutions in the post-Communist world, and the Arab Spring have often been frustrated. "History" is manifestly not over, and the forces that stand for ordered liberty in the world seem to be in retreat. Too much of Latin America has reverted to chronic patterns of corruption and authoritarianism, or corruption and incompetence, or corruption, incompetence, and authoritarianism. Incapable of putting its fiscal house in order, responding forcefully to the threats posed by a revanchist Russia, or dealing with home-brewed jihadist terrorism and anti-Semitism, Europe remains paralyzed by a crisis of civilizational morale that only the willfully ignorant or fanatically secular will fail to recognize as spiritual in character. That religious freedom has come under assault in the West within two decades of its vindication in the formerly Communist world was not something that many expected in 1989— or at the turn of the millennium, for that matter. What Pope Francis has aptly described as a "throwaway culture", in which the disposable are not just consumer goods but people, is eroding the moral-cultural fabric of our civilization. Drastically different ideas of the human person, human community, and human destiny are in conflict throughout the Western world and have much to do with the alleged gridlock of American domestic politics.

At such a moment, it is imperative to learn and take heart from John Paul II, and refuse to be bound by self-imposed shackles of low expectations, submitting to the tyranny of the possible as the conventional wisdom of the day defines the possible. Had Karol Wojtyła, on becoming John Paul II, accepted the conventional wisdom of the moment, he would have settled down to manage the inevitable decline of the Catholic Church in a world permanently divided along geopolitical and ideological fault lines defined in the late 1940s. Because he believed more deeply, and thus saw more clearly, he discerned sources of renewal in the Church where others saw only decay, and he saw openings for freedom where others saw only impenetrable walls. By refusing to accept the tyranny of the possible, he helped make what seemed impossible not only possible but real.

Events proved that his signature challenge on October 22, 1978, during the inauguration of his pontificate ("Be not afraid!") was not romanticism. It was the deepest, truest realism. Or as he put it to thousands of young people in Kraków in June 1979, as they gathered near the site of the martyrdom of Saint Stanislaus, "Be afraid only of thoughtlessness and pusillanimity." That summons and that challenge remain entirely salient, four decades later.

# Reading Regensburg Right

## Benedict XVI on the Dilemma of Islam and Political Modernity

On the night of September 12, 2006, my wife and I were dining with two of Pope John Paul II's oldest friends in their Cracovian home when my mobile phone began ringing. It was an agitated Italian reporter who got immediately to the point: "Zee Pope has just given zees crazee *conferenza* in Germania about zee Muslims. What do you zay about it?" I said that I couldn't answer as I hadn't read Pope Benedict XVI's lecture. "*Sì, sì,* I know," my caller responded, "but what do you *zay* about it?" I then replied that, unlike some of my caller's countrymen—indeed, unlike some of my own—I wasn't in the habit of commenting on papal texts until I had read them; so would he please e-mail me a copy of the text so that I could read it on the plane home the next day, at which point he could call me back for a comment. This he did, which in turn led to my conducting a trans-Atlantic telephone interview from the Wendy's at Newark Liberty International Airport.

I recount this minor journalistic melodrama in order to lay down two preliminary markers.

First, from the moment I finished reading it, Benedict XVI's September 12, 2006, lecture given at the University of Regensburg, Germany, struck me as one of the most important papal statements on public matters of global consequence since John Paul II's address to the United Nations General Assembly in October 1995. In the latter, John Paul defended the universality of human rights on the basis of a universal human nature, from which could be read a universal moral law. Absent a universal human nature and a universal moral law that could be known by the disciplined exercise of reason, John Paul argued, there could be no universal conversation about universal goods, no universal consideration of the human future. And absent a universal moral law functioning as a kind of cross-cultural grammar for ordering a genuine dialogue, there would only be noise—cacophony. John Paul II's 1995 U.N. address thus identified one set of pressing issues for the immediate post–Cold War period; Benedict XVI's Regensburg Lecture, in turn, clearly identified a cluster of related and equally pressing issues underlying the new world disorder of the early twenty-first century.

Second, the initial media reaction to Regensburg—"The Pope made a gaffe!"—got set in quick-drying cement and remained there throughout his pontificate, at least as a default position in the world press. When the agenda for Pope Benedict's April 2008 visit to the United States was released, more than a few media outlets mentioned the Regensburg misstep, as they continued to construe it. In the immediate aftermath of Regensburg, my colleagues and I published several op-ed columns and articles in a number of newspapers and newsmagazines arguing that Benedict XVI knew exactly what he was saying, and that if his critics would do him the courtesy of reading the text in its entirety, they might come to a similar conclusion. We also argued that there wasn't a centimeter's worth of difference between Benedict XVI's theological reading of Islam and John Paul II's—a gap between the two popes being another antiphon in the chorus of deprecation by which "God's Rottweiler" was being transformed into God's Dunce. All that this effort at explanation managed to accomplish, in my case, was to increase the volume of e-mail I was receiving with slightly disconcerting subject lines like "Greetings from Peshawar; we are unhappy with you."

Reading Regensburg right requires clearing away some of this rubble, in order to assess the claim that Regensburg was, in fact, a critically important papal statement correctly identifying one of the mega dynamics of early twenty-first-century history, and in order to see how the Regensburg Lecture could help set the foundation for a genuine, truth-centered dialogue of cultures.

To begin with the alleged "gaffe", there was much left to be desired in the way the Holy See's often-clumsy communications apparatus handled Regensburg. The press was not properly briefed on what to expect from the Pope's lecture and on why he was saying what he was saying. The post-lecture controversy was not anticipated, and so an adequate menu of responses was not ready to hand. It took more than a week for the Vatican to post the complete text of the Regensburg Lecture, including its scholarly apparatus, on its website.

The net effect of this Italianate fumbling around was to reinforce the impression that a gaffe had indeed been made, that the Pope had indeed "misspoken", and that amends had to be made so that interreligious comity could be restored (hence the hastily arranged meeting between the Pope and the diplomatic representatives of several Islamic states at Castel Gandolfo in late September 2006). How anything the Pope said at Regensburg gave reasonable cause for the lethally violent reactions to the lecture, once the jihadists had gotten the Regensburg bit into their teeth, was left unexplored by the media. Jihadists do not, of course, march to the Holy See's drummer; but one has to ask whether a more adroit management of the immediate post-lecture controversy by the Holy See might not have dampened passions to the point where they could not be so successfully (and, it would seem, readily) ignited.

Yet it still beggars belief to give credence to the claim that Benedict XVI, a man with a half-century's experience of public controversy, did not know what he was saying at Regensburg. It further beggars belief to give credence to the suggestion that he was being deliberately provocative, even insulting.

First of all, Benedict XVI has always been a Christian gentleman whose exquisite manners reflect both his innate shyness and his deep-seated respect for others. He is incapable of the gratuitous insult. He was also a man acutely aware of his responsibilities as pope, which included the papal *sollicitudo omnium ecclesiarum*, the papal "solicitude for all the churches", which includes persecuted churches like the hard-pressed churches in Islamic states. The "Rottweiler" caricature of Benedict XVI, vicious and inaccurate but still lurking in the subconscious of some journalists, was an interpretive filter distorting the message of Regensburg.

Secondly, the "gaffe" hermeneutic on Regensburg must contend with Benedict XVI's encyclopedic knowledge of theology, which ranges far beyond Catholic thought to encompass Protestant and Orthodox thinking, Jewish scholarship, and Islamic commentators.

Benedict XVI is not, of course, as well-versed in some of these disciplines as he is in others. But he is certainly not ignorant of the main currents of thought in other world religious traditions, as some of the post-Regensburg commentary suggested.

Then, in the third place, there is the precision of his mind. I have been blessed by the acquaintance of many brilliant men and women. Benedict XVI is one of the very, very few brilliant people I have ever known who when asked a question, pauses, reflects, and *then* answers in complete paragraphs—and in his third or fourth language. He says precisely what he means and means exactly what he says. And if that was true of his performance as cardinal during interviews and conversations in his office at the Congregation for the Doctrine of the Faith, how much more would it be true of his performance in a rather formal academic context such as the Regensburg Lecture?

Thus the notion of Regensburg-as-papal-"gaffe" is prima facie implausible.

What, then, did this precise man say in his Regensburg Lecture? Benedict's first point was that all the great questions of life, including social and political questions, are ultimately theological. How we think (or don't think) about God has much to do with how we think about what is good and what is wicked, how we judge what is noble and what is base, and how we think about the appropriate methods for advancing the truth in a world in which there are profound disagreements about the truth of things.

If, for example, men and women imagine God to be pure will, an absolutely transcendent and inapproachable dominance to whom the only appropriate response is submission, then there will be little room within our theology for a God of reason, a God of "Logos"— and still less room for a God of love. A God of radical willfulness can command anything, even the irrational. To be sure, there have been Christian thinkers (Scotus and Ockham, for starters) who have tended to imagine God this way: pure will, pure dominance. But their views are in considerable theological tension with the mainstream of the Christian tradition, in which the God of the Bible is a God of reason and love, a God who comes searching for man in history and invites human beings into a dialogue of salvation. As Saint Augustine has said, this is the God for whom our hearts are restless, until they rest in his embrace.

This God cannot command the unreasonable, for to do so would be to contradict his own nature. This theological datum yields an important anthropological by-product that has shaped Christian moral reflection on the right ordering of society for centuries. For in the human capacity for reason, we see the imprint of the divine reason, the "Logos", the Word through whom the world was made. Thus God's self-revelation—first to the people of Israel, later and definitively in his Son—does not "cancel" human reason: God's revelation appeals to human reason, to the divine spark within us. That is why mainstream Christianity has always taught that human beings can build decent societies by attending to reason. That is why natural law ways of thinking about the good have helped shape Christian reflection on society, on war and peace, and on politics for centuries.

Thus Benedict XVI's first point is that our idea of God inevitably influences our ideas of theology and politics.

Benedict's second point followed closely on his first: irrational violence aimed at innocent men, women, and children is, as he put it at Regensburg, "incompatible with the nature of God and the nature of the soul". Pope Benedict was certainly not laying down a blanket indictment here; he would, I am confident, agree that it is very much worth engaging in the most serious of scholarly conversations in order to clarify and explore the several theologies of God at work in the complex worlds-within-worlds of Islam. But while that exploration is under way, it is equally imperative to recognize, as Benedict did at Regensburg, that certain currents of thought in contemporary Islam insist (to take the most dramatic and odious example) that the suicide bombing of innocents is an act pleasing to God: an act of martyrdom meriting eternal bliss. Muting the latter point cannot be the admission ticket for engaging the deeper dialogue about the divine nature. Moreover, it is the responsibility of all who worship the one true God to declare, unambiguously, that the murder of innocents in the name of advancing the divine cause in the world is an abomination based on gravely mistaken understandings about God, about God's will and God's purposes, and about the nature of moral obligation.

To be sure, responsibility for challenging these distorted views of God and the distorted understanding of moral duty that flows from them rests, first, with Islamic leaders. But too few Islamic leaders have been willing to undertake a cleansing of Islam's conscience in the way that John Paul II taught the Catholic Church to cleanse its historical conscience in preparation for the Great Jubilee of 2000. We know that, in the past, Christians used violence to advance Christian purposes. The Catholic Church has publicly repented of such distortions of the Gospel and has developed a deep theological critique of the misunderstandings that led to such episodes. Can the Church, therefore, be of some help to those brave Islamic reformers who, at the risk of their own lives, are trying to develop a parallel Islamic critique of their co-religionists' misunderstandings?

By citing a robust exchange between a medieval Byzantine emperor and a learned Islamic scholar—the quotation that got the world media into a frenzy—Benedict XVI was not making a cheap rhetorical point; he was trying to illustrate the possibility of a tough-minded but rational dialogue between Christians and Muslims. That dialogue can take place, however, only on the basis of a shared commitment to reason and a mutual rejection of irrational violence in the name of God.

Pope Benedict's third point, which was almost entirely ignored in the years since the Regensburg Lecture—although he later elaborated it in lectures in Paris, London, and Berlin—was directed to the West. If the high culture of the West continues to fritter its time away in the intellectual sandbox of postmodern irrationalism, in which there is "your truth" and "my truth" but nothing properly describable as "the truth", the West will be unable to defend itself. Why? Because the West won't be able to give reasons why its commitments to civility, tolerance, human rights, and the rule of law are worth defending. A Western world stripped of convictions about the truths that make Western civilization possible cannot make a useful contribution to a genuine dialogue of civilizations and cultures, for any such dialogue must be based on a shared understanding that human beings can, however imperfectly, come to know the truth of things.

Can Islam be self-critical? Can its leaders condemn and marginalize its extremists, or are Muslims condemned to be held hostage to the passions of those who consider the murder of innocents to be pleasing to God? Can the West recover its commitment to reason and thus help support Islamic reformers? These were the large questions that Benedict XVI tried to put on the world's agenda at Regensburg. No one else could have done so: no president, prime minister, king, queen, or secretary-general could put these questions into play, at this level of sophistication, and for a world audience. But Benedict XVI did more than raise unavoidable questions at Regensburg; he also gave the political world a grammar for addressing these questions: the genuinely cross-cultural grammar of rationality and irrationality. The theological communities of the great world religious traditions can conduct a robust interreligious dialogue within their own specialist grammars and vocabularies. Something other than those specialist grammars and vocabularies is required in public life. The grammar of "rationality/irrationality" just might be that "something".

The *National Catholic Reporter* editorially criticized the Regensburg Lecture as having trafficked "too much in theological abstraction". Pope Benedict did precisely the opposite; at Regensburg, Benedict XVI did the world an immense service by giving believers and nonbelievers alike a language with which to deal with the threat of jihadist ideology: the language of rationality and irrationality. Far from being an exercise in "theological abstraction", the Regensburg Lecture was a courageous attempt to create a new public grammar capable of disciplining and directing the world's discussion of what is inarguably one of the world's gravest problems.

And in doing these things, Benedict XVI was in sync with the view of Islam, its religious accomplishments, and its challenges held by his predecessor, John Paul II.

In the wake of the Regensburg Lecture, it was (at the least) ironic to hear some of the same voices that used to lament the "hard-line" and "conservative" Polish Pope now lifting John Paul up as a paragon of enlightened, benign liberality—ironic, perhaps even amusing, but slightly disconcerting. More disconcerting, however, were the attempts to drive a wedge between Benedict and his papal predecessor by those who could care less about internal Catholic debates, but who saw their chance to make a seemingly decisive point and took it. Thus in the aftermath of Regensburg the Arabic satellite TV network Al Jazeera ran a series of cartoons featuring a John Paul figure releasing peaceful doves in St. Peter's Square; the doves are then shot down by Benedict from the roof of the Bernini colonnade surrounding the Square. The last images in the series have John Paul weeping, head in hands, while Benedict, holding a smoking shotgun, smirks.

All of which is silly and vulgar, of course. But it isn't that far from the views expressed by some Catholics, lamenting what they allege to be the drastic difference between Wojtyła's and Ratzinger's views of Islam.

The 1994 international best seller *Crossing the Threshold of Hope* was John Paul II's most personal statement, a summary of his convictions about faith, prayer, the papal mission, other world religions, and the human future. As such, it has a special claim on our attention as an expression of Karol Wojtyła's views, which were honed by an acute intelligence and a long experience of the world. One section of *Threshold* is devoted to Islam. In it, John Paul expressed his respect for "the religiosity of Muslims" and his admiration for their "fidelity to prayer". As the late pope put it, "The image of believers in Allah who, without caring about time or place, fall to their knees and immerse themselves in prayer remains a model for all those who invoke the true God, in particular for those Christians who, having deserted their magnificent cathedrals, pray only a little or not at all."

But do these expressions of respect suggest, as *National Public Radio*'s Sylvia Poggioli did after Regensburg, that John Paul II (in marked contrast to Benedict XVI) had put Islam "on the same plane" as Catholicism? Hardly. Here, again, is the authentic voice of John Paul II, from *Crossing the Threshold of Hope*:

> Whoever knows the Old and New Testaments, and then reads the Koran, clearly sees the process by which it completely reduces Divine Revelation. It is impossible not to note the movement away from what God said about himself, first in the Old Testament through the Prophets, and then finally in the New Testament through His Son. In Islam, all the richness of God's self-revelation, which constitutes the heritage of the Old and New Testaments, has definitely been set aside.
>
> Some of the most beautiful names in human language are given to the God of the Koran, but He is ultimately a God outside of the world, a God who is only Majesty, never Emmanuel, God with us. Islam is not a religion of redemption. There is no room for the Cross and the Resurrection. Jesus is mentioned, but only as a prophet who prepares for the last prophet, Muhammad. There is also mention of Mary, His Virgin Mother, but the tragedy of redemption is completely absent. For this reason not only the theology but also the anthropology of Islam is very distant from Christianity.

That was the personal testimony of John Paul II, which is in some respects more blunt and challenging than anything Benedict XVI said at Regensburg. But we can leave the comparisons and contrasts for another day. The point here is that there isn't a centimeter of difference between John Paul II's substantive evaluation of Islam and Benedict XVI's. John Paul II was a master of the public gesture; but to read from his public gestures of respect for Islamic piety an agreement with Islam's understanding of God, man, and moral obligation is to make a grave mistake. John Paul II would have completely agreed with Benedict XVI's critique at Regensburg of any theology that reduces God to pure will, the remote, divine dictator who can command the irrational (like the murder of innocents) if he chooses. And, like Benedict XVI, John Paul II knew that such misconceptions can have lethal public consequences, because all the great questions of the human condition, including political questions, are ultimately theological.

Benedict XVI bore the burden of the papacy at a historical moment in which religiously warranted irrationality was a lethal threat to the future of civilization. He and his predecessor had the same view of the theological conditions for the possibility of that irrationality. What Benedict added to the mix is a broader analysis of the problem of faith and reason as engaging the West (a theme, to be sure, also found in John Paul II) and a prescription for the direction the dialogue over faith and reason should take.

Benedict XVI elaborated that analysis in his Christmas 2006 address to the Roman Curia.

These annual addresses, framed by a formal exchange of greetings between the pope and his senior collaborators, are often used by popes to review the year just past and to provide some clues as to themes to be developed in the year ahead. Late 2006 had been an especially busy period, between Regensburg and the papal pilgrimage to the Ecumenical Patriarchate of Constantinople. Benedict XVI, reflecting on both experiences and the controversies that had attended them, had the following to say:

> In a dialogue to be intensified with Islam, we must bear in mind the fact that the Muslim world today is finding itself faced with an

urgent task. This task is very similar to the one that was imposed upon Christians since the Enlightenment, and to which the Second Vatican Council, as the fruit of long and difficult research, found real solutions for the Catholic Church....

It is a question of the attitude that the community of the faithful must adopt in the face of the convictions and demands that were strengthened in the Enlightenment.

On the one hand, one must counter a dictatorship of positivist reason that excludes God from the life of the community and from public organizations....

On the other hand, one must welcome the true conquests of the Enlightenment, human rights, and especially the freedom of faith and its practice, and recognize these also as being essential elements for the authenticity of religion.

As in the Christian community, where there has been a long search to find the correct position of faith in relation to such beliefs—a search that will certainly never be concluded once and for all—so also the Islamic world with its own tradition faces the immense task of finding the appropriate solutions to these problems.

The content of the dialogue between Christians and Muslims will be at this time especially one of meeting each other in this commitment to find the right solutions. We Christians feel ourselves in solidarity with all those who, precisely on the basis of their religious convictions as Muslims, work to oppose violence and for the synergy between faith and reason, between religion and freedom.

Thus in his own authoritative commentary on the Regensburg Lecture (and to translate from Vatican English to standard English), Benedict XVI suggested the following.

First, history itself has put before the Islamic world the "urgent task" of finding a way to come to grips with the intellectual and institutional achievements of the Enlightenment—the Muslim world can no longer live as if the Enlightenment, in both its achievements and its flaws, had not happened. The intra-Islamic civil war over these questions has now spilled out of the House of Islam and now affects the entire world. That blunt fact of twenty-first-century public life underscores the urgency of the task facing Islam's religious leaders and legal scholars.

Second, this necessary Islamic encounter with Enlightenment thought and the institutions of governance that grew out of it requires separating the Enlightenment wheat from the Enlightenment chaff. The skepticism and relativism that characterize one stream of Enlightenment thought need not (and should not) be accepted. Yet one can (and must) make a distinction between the ideas that the Enlightenment got right—religious freedom, understood as an inalienable human right to be acknowledged and protected by any just government, and the separation of political and religious authority in the state—even as one rejects the ideas of which the Enlightenment made a hash: for example, the idea of God.

Third, this process of coming to grips with the complex heritage and continuing momentum of the Enlightenment is an ongoing one. As the twentieth-century experience of the Catholic Church demonstrated in recent decades, however, an ancient religious tradition can appropriate certain aspects of Enlightenment thought as a means of clarifying its own deep convictions and can come to appreciate the institutions of freedom that emerged from the Enlightenment, without compromising in a fundamental way its core theological commitments. Indeed, the experience of the Catholic Church on the question of religious freedom and the institutional separation of church and state shows that a serious, critical engagement with Enlightenment ideas and institutions can lead a religious community to a revivification of classic theological concepts that may have lain dormant for a long period of time, and thus to a genuine development of religious understanding.

The Catholic Church came to the understandings embodied in *Dignitatis Humanae*, the Second Vatican Council's Declaration on Religious Freedom, not by a Jacobin kicking-over of the theological traces, but by a process of retrieval and development that brought ancient, if long-forgotten, elements of the faith and of Christian philosophy into conversation with modern public life. Might this process of retrieval and development hold some lessons for our Muslim interlocutors?

Fourth, it is precisely on this ground, the ground where faith meets reason in a search for the truth about how just societies should be structured, that interreligious dialogue should be constructed.

Thus in Benedict XVI's view, the interreligious dialogue of the future should focus on helping those Muslims willing to do so to explore the possibility of an *Islamic* case for religious tolerance, social pluralism, and civil society, even as Islam's interlocutors (among Christians, Jews, and others, including nonbelievers) open themselves to the possibility that the Islamic critique of certain aspects of modern culture is not without merit.

That seems right. While no one should preclude the possibility of a genuine theological dialogue between "Islam and the rest" on important theological questions—the nature of God; the mode of God's engagement with his world; Islamic supersessionism and the resulting Islamic conception of both Judaism and Christianity; a critical understanding of the history of sacred texts and a proper method for their exegesis—the most urgent, immediate questions for a dialogue of cultures between Islam and the West, and specifically between Islam and Catholicism, engage issues of practical reason, such as the organization of twenty-first-century societies and relations within the twenty-first-century global commons. The deeper theological dialogue with Islam is a dialogue whose progress, if such is possible, will be measured in centuries. The dialogue proposed by Benedict XVI is one with an immediate urgency about it.

As the Pope reminded the Curia, Catholicism spent the better part of two centuries trying to find solutions to the questions of faith, freedom, and governance posed by the Enlightenment, a process that bore fruit at the Second Vatican Council. Isn't this theological method of retrieval and renewal a useful model for a Christian-Islamic dialogue? For unless Islam can find within its own spiritual and legal resources an Islamic way to legitimate religious freedom (or at least religious toleration) and the distinction between religious and political authority, the relationship between the world's 2.3 billion Christians and its 1.8 billion Muslims is going to remain fraught with tension.

A dialogue about the human future, the structuring of international public life, and the encounter of Christian and Islamic cultures that does not begin, even tacitly, from the fact that one of the dialogue partners has (if with difficulty) assimilated the genuine achievements of the Enlightenment in the sphere of governance, while the other has not, is not a conversation likely to be fruitful. Indeed, it is a dialogue likely to engage precisely the wrong Islamic interlocutors.

Reading Regensburg right, therefore, requires us to grasp the public implications of Benedict's analysis of the complex crisis of faith and reason in the first decades of the twenty-first century. That crisis, as the Pope acutely observed in his lecture, is being played out *within* the West and *within* the Islamic world, as well as *between* the West and Islam. If there is a nodal point at which these three dimensions of the crisis of faith and reason intersect, it is on the question of religious freedom, and on the question of what is required, culturally, to create the kind of societies that can warrant, sustain, and defend religious freedom in full. Thus any dialogue of cultures that fails to address the question of religious freedom will dissolve ultimately—and perhaps rapidly—into a dialogue of the deaf.

Winston Churchill, who did not shrink from war when war became necessary, famously said that "jaw, jaw is better than war, war." That is certainly true. But it is just as true that a false kind of dialogue in which the engagement of differences within the bond of civility is displaced by political correctness, historical self-deprecation, and a failure to identity the roots of competing perceptions of human goods yields a kind of "jaw, jaw" that is, in fact, "blah, blah"—a false dialogue that brings us no closer to the peace that is the fruit of order, an order that is itself an expression of moral reason.

Pope Benedict XVI's Regensburg Lecture, read with open minds and open hearts, could, even now, help initiate a true interreligious dialogue. It is past time to get on with that urgent task.

Part Two

# A Republic in Disarray

# Truths Still Held?

## *The Murray Template and American Political Culture*

John Courtney Murray's *We Hold These Truths: Catholic Reflections on the American Proposition*, first published in 1960, remains one of the most important such studies ever composed. Its appearance landed Father Murray, an urbane New York Jesuit, on the cover of *Time*, in the days when that distinction meant something. Three years later, New York's Francis Cardinal Spellman brought Murray to the Second Vatican Council as a *peritus*, a theological adviser, so that Murray's work on church-state theory could help shape the Council's deliberations on religious liberty, an issue of particular concern to the bishops of the United States.

For a man who was America's most prominent Catholic public intellectual in 1965, the year in which Vatican II adopted the Declaration on Religious Freedom that his thought had helped make possible, Murray went into rapid eclipse after his untimely death in 1967 from a long-standing heart ailment. The younger Jesuit generation jettisoned Murray as impossibly old hat, claiming, as one put it, that "we know so much more than Murray did." In the mid-1980s, however, after twenty years of neglect, Murray was resurrected by Catholic thinkers seeking materials from which to build a religiously informed public philosophy for the American experiment in ordered liberty. This, in turn, led to an effort, perhaps not surprising, to reclaim Murray for progressive Catholicism—a project risible to anyone familiar with the stories of Murray's contempt for some of the woollier-headed liberal notions being circulated at Woodstock College in the years before his death.

*We Hold These Truths* was not without its critics, both in the 1960s and more recently. Some have argued that Murray's account of the

American founding massively reduced the role of biblical religion, and especially Calvinism, in the national consensus that produced the new republic. Others have suggested that Murray's theory of democracy was based on an excessively neo-Scholastic (meaning, specifically, Suarezian) reading of the relation between nature and grace, even as others have argued that Murray's theory of democracy is too beholden to John Locke. Then there are the critics who find in Murray an opening for what might be called Cuomoism among Catholic public officials—a charge that does a disservice to Murray even as it gives an undeserved intellectual gloss to Mario Cuomo and those theologians and lawyers who helped turn Catholic politicians into advocates for "reproductive choice".

My purpose here is not to sort out the arguments over Murray's analysis of the founding, and still less to judge the metaphysics and epistemology that buttressed his church-state theory. Rather, I want to review the "American Proposition" he sketched in *We Hold These Truths* because it offers a useful template for measuring the health of the American republic and its political culture in the twenty-first century.

The opening paragraphs of Murray's book summarize its argument and give the flavor of his cool, dry rhetorical style:

> It is classic American doctrine, immortally asserted by Abraham Lincoln, that the new nation which our Fathers brought forth on this continent was dedicated to a "proposition."
>
> In philosophy, a proposition is the statement of a truth to be demonstrated. In mathematics, a proposition is at times the statement of an operation to be performed. Our Fathers dedicated the nation to a proposition in both of those senses. The American proposition is at once both doctrinal and practical, a theorem and a problem. It is an affirmation and also an intention. It presents itself as a coherent structure of thought [even as] it also presents itself as an organized political project that aims at historical success....
>
> Neither as a doctrine nor as a project is the American Proposition a finished thing. Its demonstration is never done once for all; and the Proposition itself requires development on penalty of decadence. Its historical success is never to be taken for granted, nor can it come to some absolute term; and any given measure of success demands

enlargement on penalty of instant decline. In a moment of national crisis Lincoln asserted the imperiled part of the theorem and gave impetus to the impeded part of the project in the noble utterance, at once declaratory and imperative, "All men are created equal." Today, when civil war has become the basic fact of world society, there is no element of the theorem that is not menaced by active negation, and no thrust of the project that does not meet powerful opposition. Today therefore thoughtful men among us are saying that America must be more clearly conscious of what it proposes, more articulate in proposing, more purposeful in the realization of the project proposed.

The American Proposition, as Murray understood it, was a conservation by development of the political dimension of Western civilization as it emerged over the centuries from the culturally fruitful interaction of Jerusalem, Athens, and Rome—that is, the interaction of biblical religion, Greek rationality, and Roman law. As such, the Proposition rested on a realist approach to reason and personal reflection: there are truths built into the world and into us; we can know those truths through the arts of reason; that knowledge lays certain obligations, both personal and civil, on us. To be sure, those truths had to be "held, assented to, worked into the texture of institutions" for there to be a "true City, in which men may dwell in dignity, peace, unity, justice, well-being, [and] freedom". But that never-to-be-taken-for-granted quality of the truths of the American Proposition simply underscored the fact that the United States was an experiment—an experiment in ordered freedom.

That could be said, I suppose, of any democracy; Weimar Germany and the French Third Republic chillingly demonstrate the perils attending any democracy's failure to order its public life by the moral truths we can know by reason. What is distinctive about American democracy, however, is that our very nationhood depended on the truths to which the Founders pledged their lives, fortunes, and sacred honor. The German nation remained Germany after the collapse of the Weimar Republic; France remained France under the Vichy regime. But, Murray argued, America's native condition was plurality, and the American people—the American *nation*—had to be constructed, not out of the old materials of blood and ethnicity and language and soil and common religious conviction, but out of the new materials of adherence to truths in the civic order. The survival of America, as both theorem and project, rested on the American ability to create *pluralism* out of plurality—that is, to transform the cacophony of ethnic and religious difference into an orderly conversation about public goods, based on a common allegiance to the elementary truths of the Proposition.

Murray's theory of democracy, while seeming thin to some of his critics, was thus far thicker than that of today's democratic functionalists, whose sole concern is to get the machinery of governance right. Murray, by contrast, thought of politics not as machinery but as deliberation—common deliberation among men and women who were citizens and not merely bundles of desires; common deliberation about public goods, using the arts of reason to apply agreed-on first principles of truth in the civic order to the demands of governance amid the flux of history. In this conception of democracy, civility and tolerance are moral accomplishments, not poses, attitudes, or pragmatic accommodations. Tolerance means not differences ignored but differences engaged. Civility is the achievement of order (and thus a measure of clarity and perhaps even charity) in the public conversation.

"The distinctive bond" of civil society, Murray wrote, "is reason, or, more exactly, that exercise of reason which is argument." Argument, in turn, gave form to a distinctive kind of association in the American democratic experiment. Jacques Maritain might have called it "civic friendship". A generation after Murray, John Paul II called it "solidarity". It is, Murray wrote, a "special kind of moral virtue, a thing of reason and intelligence, laboriously cultivated by the [disciplining] of passion, prejudice, and narrow self-interest." This is not the friendship of David and Jonathan, or the fierce inclusiveness of the clan or tribe; it is not the bond of charity that binds disciples within the communion of the Church. It is a civic friendship and solidarity born of a common passion for justice, with the requirements of justice—what is owed by the city to the citizenry, and what citizens owe the city—understood according to the canons of public reason.

The bonds of this civic friendship in America reinforced the founding consensus that gave philosophical content to Murray's American Proposition. This consensus was, in Murray's words, "an ensemble of substantive truths, a structure of basic knowledge, an order of elementary affirmations" that reflect the truths we can and must know by reason about how we ought to live together. No political arrangement is possible if everything is in doubt. If there is to be genuine argument, Murray wrote, there must be "a core of agreement, accord, concurrence, acquiescence".

This may sound daunting, but we need not discover these truths by our own labors alone. Rather, the truths that form the moral-cultural foundations of American democracy come to us, as an inheritance to be honored and cultivated, from the project of Western civilization: the gift that Leo XIII, founder of modern Catholic social doctrine, called the patrimony of mankind.

The first of these inherited truths that give content to the American Proposition is that we are a nation under judgment, because God is sovereign over nations as well as individuals, a fact that "lies beyond politics", Murray insisted, and "imparts to politics a fundamental human meaning". Here, like Edmund Burke, Murray distinguished the Anglo-American political tradition from the Jacobinism of Continental European political philosophy. The latter began its thinking about politics with autonomous human reason; the former looked "to the sovereignty of God as to the first principle of its organization". The American experiment, in other words, was an experiment under transcendent judgment—the judgment of the God of the Bible, the judgment of those moral truths inscribed by nature's God into the world and into us, as a reflection of the divine creative purpose.

That "natural law", which we can know by reason, gives government the authority to command, even as it limits the power of governors. The constitutional agreement by which the people, through their representatives, ratified the basic instruments of American governance and amended that agreement as circumstances required created a process, as Murray understood it, by which "the people define the areas where [public] authority is legitimate and the areas where liberty is lawful".

The second foundational truth of the American Proposition also grew out of the Christian Middle Ages: the principle that all just governance exists *by* and *with* the consent of the governed. On this reading of Western history, royal absolutism and its parallel union of altar and throne were an aberration; the rich social pluralism of the Middle Ages and the assumed limits on princely authority reflect, in Murray's view, "the premise ... that there is a sense of justice inherent in the people". This principle of consent, with its premise that the people can know the moral truths by which we ought to live together, stands in sharp contrast to the Jacobin tradition in Continental Europe and its twentieth-century manifestation in totalitarianism, which proposed governance by elite vanguards.

The principle of consent and the premise of the people's sense of justice framed Murray's understanding of human rights, which posed another challenge to an autonomy-based theory of democracy:

> The proper premise of these freedoms lay in the fact that they were social necessities.... They were regarded as conditions essential to the conduct of free, representative, and responsible government. People who are called upon to obey have the right first to be heard. People who are to bear burdens and make sacrifices have the right first to pronounce on the purposes which their sacrifices serve. People who are summoned to contribute to the common good have the right first to pass their own judgment on the question, whether the good proposed be truly a good, the people's good.

In the American Proposition, in other words, rights are not trumps recognized as such by the sheer fact of their assertion. Rather, rights are rooted in the dignity of the human person as capable of rational moral choice and considered political judgment. Thus, rights are acknowledged in law to facilitate the promotion and defense of human dignity and of the common good, not simply to innoculate individual "choice" from what someone may consider "interference".

The third truth of the American Proposition is, as Murray put it, that "the state is distinct from society and limited in its offices toward society." Society exists prior to the state, ontologically as well as historically, and the state exists to serve society, not the other way around. This retrieval of the medieval distinction between *studium* and *imperium*, the order of culture and the political order, would have large consequences for Murray's church-state theory and indeed for the Second Vatican Council, but in the American

Experiment, the salient point, as Murray put it, was that government, rightly understood, "submits itself to judgment by the truth of society; it is not itself a judge of the truth in society". Neither is government the judge of the truths inscribed in nature. Rightly ordered government submits itself to the judgment of those truths built into the world and into us, and if it attempts to redefine those truths, it has acted unjustly and illegitimately.

The fourth component of the American Proposition is "the profound conviction that only a virtuous people can be free". Murray knew that there are no guarantees about the success of freedom. Freedom can dissipate into license, private license into public decadence, decadence into chaos, and chaos into authoritarianism. "It is not an American belief," Murray wrote, that "free government is inevitable, only that it is possible." Moreover, "its possibility can be realized only when the people as a whole are inwardly governed by the recognized imperatives of the universal moral law." Freedom and moral truth, Murray wrote in anticipation of the teaching of John Paul II in *Centesimus Annus*, are inextricably bound together: freedom must be tethered to truth and ordered to goodness if freedom is not to become its own undoing.

Murray applauded the ways in which the American cultural instinct for freedom had succeeded in placing limits on the sphere of government within a functioning democracy. But the American demand for freedom could "be made with the full resonance of moral authority only to the extent that it issues from an inner sense of responsibility to a higher law". The American idea is *ordered* freedom: ordered to goodness because it is tethered to truth. "Men who would be free politically must discipline themselves," Murray explained. "Political freedom is endangered in its foundations as soon as the universal moral values, upon whose shared possession the self-discipline of a free society depends, are no longer vigorous enough to restrain the passions and shatter the selfish inertia of men." Democracy, in other words, is "a spiritual and moral enterprise".

This was the inherited cultural consensus that, in John Courtney Murray's view, had informed and shaped the American Proposition for centuries. But were these truths still held in Murray's time, almost six decades ago? Murray had his doubts.

He did not think the Proposition could be carried any longer by the primary institutions of its historical transmission, the Christian communities of the old Protestant mainline, already beset by theological and doctrinal chaos. Nor would the falling torch be picked up by an American academy then in thrall to the philosophy of pragmatism, an academy that had "long ago bade a quiet goodbye to the whole notion of an American consensus, as implying that there are truths that we hold in common, and a natural law that makes known to all of us the structure of the moral universe in such wise that all of us are bound by it to a common obedience".

Murray's suggestion—a striking one at its historical moment, given the anti-Catholic prejudice manifest during the 1960 presidential campaign—was that the originating and constituting consensus of America was still possessed by, and might be revived by, the Catholic community in the United States. That revitalization was not to happen, as American Catholicism lurched into the fever swamps of the late 1960s and the 1970s. The opportunity Murray saw in the late 1950s and early 1960s was a victim of the post-Vatican II silly season; although if we listen carefully, we can hear echoes today, and sometimes more than echoes, of the consensus ideas of the American Proposition in the pro-life advocacy of Catholics and their allies among the more thoughtful leadership of evangelical Protestants.

On the first page of *We Hold These Truths*, Murray wrote of the "civil war" that was the "basic fact of world society". He was referring, of course, to the contest between the West and Communist totalitarianism, a contest concluded in Europe in 1989–1991. Yet the civil war, which is fundamentally anthropological in character, in that it is based on dramatically opposed ideas of the human person, continues, in what is sometimes called the American "culture war" and its analogues in Europe. Murray didn't use the term "culture war", but he clearly anticipated its possibility when he penned one of the most striking passages in his book:

> Perhaps one day the noble, many-storeyed mansion of democracy will be dismantled, leveled to the dimensions of a flat majoritarianism, which is no mansion but a barn, perhaps even a tool shed in which the weapons of tyranny may be forged. Perhaps there will one day be widespread dissent even from the political principles which emerge

from natural law. . . . The possibility that widespread dissent from these
principles should develop is not foreclosed.

Indeed not, for that possibility is now manifestly with us. But the
foreclosure need not be complete, and the mansion need not be lev-
eled or abandoned. Saving it, however, means facing squarely the
ways in which the truths of Murray's American Proposition are no
longer held.

It might seem that the first truth of the Proposition—the sovereignty of God over nations as well as individuals, with its parallel conviction about the universal moral law inscribed in nature and accessible
to reason—would be most gravely threatened by the so-called New
Atheism. But as David Bentley Hart bracingly demonstrated in *Atheist Delusions*, the attacks of Richard Dawkins, Christopher Hitchens,
Sam Harris, and Daniel Dennett do not get us to the true root of the
problem, which is not the historically ill-informed and philosophically embarrassing New Atheism, but what Romano Guardini used
to call the "interior disloyalty of modern times", which is, Murray
said, a betrayal of "the existential structure of reality itself".

This betrayal is most powerfully embodied by postmodernism's
skepticism about the human capacity to know the truth of anything
with certainty, a skepticism that yields, on the one hand, metaphysical nihilism, and, on the other hand, moral relativism. Indeed,
according to a trenchant reading of modernity by the French philosopher Rémi Brague, nihilism may be the defining challenge of this
cultural moment in the West. In Brague's analysis, the twenty-first
century will be the century of being and nothingness, as the twentieth century (defined by the contest with totalitarianism) was the
century of true and false and the nineteenth (defined by the social
question emerging from the Industrial Revolution) was the century
of good and evil. The metaphysical question—the question of loyalty
to being itself—is the cultural bottom line today, in a way not seen
since metaphysics first emerged from Greek classical philosophy.

In 1955 Flannery O'Connor wrote that "if you live today you
breathe in nihilism". Those who once found that complaint a bit
extravagant might ponder the reality of contemporary nihilism
through one of its recent public manifestations: the claim that the
natural moral law we can know by reason is, in truth, a form of

irrational bigotry and extremism. That claim was adduced on October 30, 2008, in the lead editorial of the *Washington Post*, written to cripple a candidate for attorney general of Virginia, Ken Cuccinelli, whose defense of natural law as an instrument for formulating public policy was decried by the sometimes sensible editors of the nation's leading political newspaper as a "retrofit" of "the old language of racism, bias, and intolerance".

As we assay the health of our political culture through the template of Murray's American Proposition, what was truly stunning about this editorial assault on natural law (launched in aid of the *Post*'s campaign in favor of same-sex "marriage") was its implicit willingness to throw out Jefferson's claims in the Declaration of Independence, Lincoln's claims in the Gettysburg Address, and Martin Luther King Jr.'s claims in his "Letter from Birmingham Jail", all of which appealed to a natural moral law that was a reflection of the eternal and divine law. To deny that such a moral law exists, and to compound that intellectual error by the moral crime of labeling those who still adhere to the first truth of the American Proposition as bigots, brings to mind Murray's cautions about the barbarism that threatens us: "Barbarism is not ... the forest primeval with all its relatively simple savageries. Barbarism ... is the lack of reasonable conversation according to reasonable laws."

One might think Murray's second truth—the principle of consent, which reflects the conviction that the people have an inherent sense of justice, and which is allied to the principle of participation that provides an account of the nature of our civil and political rights—is in better shape. Elections in America take place regularly, however vulgarly. Public officials are rotated in and out of office, if not as often as some would like. Initiatives and referenda can sometimes repair the damage that the people's inherent sense of justice tells them has been done to the common good by legislatures or courts. Free speech and freedom of the press are robust, if too often shallow. But the barbarians are among us on this front, too.

The most obvious instance of an assault on the principle of consent is what a 1996 *First Things* symposium termed the "judicial usurpation of politics". This violation of a constituting truth of the American Proposition was most egregious in *Roe v. Wade*; the degree to which the Supreme Court got it colossally wrong in *Roe* can be measured by the degree to which the effects of *Roe* have roiled our public life ever since. By the same token, of course, the people's refusal to acquiesce to what their inherent sense of justice tells them is the fundamental injustice embodied in America's nearly unfettered abortion license—a refusal that launched and sustains the pro-life movement—expresses the vitality of the second truth of the Proposition.

Yet it is not easy to see how the mistake that the Court made in *Roe* can be remedied until our political culture gains a firmer grip on the first truth of the Proposition. And there is a new assault on the second truth that bears careful watching and to which resistance must be mounted: the censorship of rationally defensible moral judgment in the name of laws banning what some deem "hate speech". Such censorship, enforced by coercive state power, is already under way in Canada and in Europe. The degree of resistance that can be mounted to these efforts will be an important measure of the degree to which the truth of the principle of consent is still held in these United States.

Our grasp of the third truth of the American Proposition—that the state exists to serve society, which is ontologically and historically antecedent to the state—has also become attenuated, as two recent controversies illustrate.

Debates over the doctrinal and moral boundaries of communities of faith have been a staple of American life for centuries; the state of Rhode Island is the result of one of those arguments. Into none of these debates, however, did the president of the United States ever inject himself and his office—until May 2009, when President Obama did precisely that in his commencement address at Notre Dame. There, the president leaped into the middle of a decades-long ecclesiological debate within American Catholicism by suggesting that the good Catholics, the *real* Catholics, were men like Father Theodore Hesburgh and the late Cardinal Joseph Bernardin—indeed, like all those Catholics who supported the Obama candidacy in 2008 and agreed with the president on the nature of the common ground to be sought in American public life. President Obama, in other words, would be the arbiter of authentic Catholicism in America.

The Catholic Church took care of itself during the Obama administration, in the face of many challenges. But what is worth remembering as a cautionary tale from President Obama's Notre Dame address is the speech's tone-deafness to the full meaning of religious freedom in America, which is one constitutional expression of the third truth of the American Proposition. In 2009, the White House likely thought it was simply playing wedge politics, strengthening its grip on certain Catholic constituencies while widening the gap between those Catholics and their bishops. But the larger meaning of Obama's commencement address ought not be obscured by such tactical maneuverings: here was the state, embodied by the president, claiming a purchase in what had for centuries been understood to be the inviolable territory of society.

To be sure, President Obama was not the reincarnation of the Holy Roman emperor Henry IV, contesting with the pope for the legal authority to appoint bishops. But whether or not he knew what he was doing, the president was usurping the bishops' right to define the doctrinal and moral boundaries of the Catholic community. That this astonishing act was not recognized for what it was is an important, and chilling, measure of the degree to which the third truth of the American Proposition is, at best, tenuously held these days.

Then there was and is the marriage debate. There is no need to rehearse this at length. Marriage is one of those societal institutions, like the parent-child bond, that antedate the state historically and are prior to the state ontologically and morally. Any state that redefines marriage has breached the border between society and state in a way that gravely endangers civil society and the common good. Any state that does so is engaging in what Cardinal Joseph Ratzinger called, on April 18, 2005, the "dictatorship of relativism": the use of coercive state power to compel a relativist concept of the good. Such dictatorships will, sooner or later, lead to what Pope Saint John Paul II described as "open or thinly disguised totalitarianism". *Obergefell v. Hodges*, the 2015 U.S. Supreme Court decision bringing constitutionally protected "same-sex marriage" to the entire country by one vote, was not quite-so-disguised an imposition of precisely such relativism.

As to the fourth truth within Murray's American Proposition—the truth that only a virtuous people can be free—the challenges from which it is under assault are obvious. Theories that reduce the democratic experiment to a matter of political mechanics chip away at the link between freedom and virtue by consigning virtue to the sphere of private life. The mantra of choice, the unassailable trump in our contemporary public discourse, deliberately avoids the question of the good: Choose *what*? The reduction of public virtue to an ill-defined tolerance and the use of the real f-bomb word in American politics ("fair") to shut down conversation or debate erodes our sense that civil society is built on numerous virtues. The vulgarities of contemporary popular culture—the demeaning of women by a multibillion-dollar pornography industry, the casual brutality of some aspects of our sports, the eroticism of so much advertising—are challenges to virtue and also to freedom, rightly understood. Decadence and democracy cannot indefinitely coexist. If the American experiment constantly requires new births of freedom, the birth of freedom we need in the twenty-first century is one in which freedom is once again tethered to both the true and the good.

If the Catholic community in the United States did not, in the aftermath of the Second Vatican Council and the cultural whitewater of the 1960s, grasp the destiny that Murray envisioned for it fifty years ago, might it do so today?

Any such recovery of Catholic identity and Catholic nerve would have to address America's loss of grip on the truths that constitute us as a unique and uniquely free people. The Church has been doing so for almost four decades now by insisting that the defense of the right to life of the unborn, and indeed of all innocent life from conception until natural death, is a first principle of justice that can be known by reason, regardless of one's theological location or lack thereof. More recently, the Church took up the cudgels of public argument in defense of marriage rightly understood, in defense of its own integrity as a self-governing institution, and in defense of the conscience rights of the people of the Church. These efforts must continue and they must be intensified, despite the setbacks experienced.

In addition, however, the Catholic Church in America, if it is to help rebuild the foundations of the American democratic experiment in ordered freedom, must remind America of the truths about the principle of consent, and the priority of society over the state, that are essential building blocks of American democracy. Those truths are embodied in what modern Catholic social doctrine calls the principle of subsidiarity. According to this principle, the Church lifts up and honors those mediating institutions or voluntary associations that stand between the individual and the state, and teaches that decision-making should be left at the lowest possible level of society—that is, at the level of those most directly affected by the decision, commensurate with the common good.

These mediating institutions and that rich pluralism of societal deliberation and decision-making constitute what John Paul II called the "subjectivity of society". Both the institutions and the pluralism are threatened today by the seemingly inexhorable thrust of the modern state into every crevice of life. Were the Church to take on this essential task of public moral education, some reconsideration of long-standing Catholic policy positions as articulated by the bishops of the United States might be required; how, for example, is it possible to achieve universal health care while honoring the principle of subsidiarity? If the principle of subsidiarity is true, then there must be answers to this question and to related questions in the fields of education and social welfare that do not involve a wholesale transfer of power to the national government. The search for those answers, which may well lie in a reconception of the roles of both government and mediating institutions, ought to help in the process of regrounding American public life in two of its foundational truths.

There are occasional, if all too often feeble, signs that the dictatorship of relativism is being challenged in American public life by the advocates of classical biblical morality and classical Western political philosophy. Yet Murray's template reminds us to be ever attentive to the deeper, long-term trends in our political culture. And amid the turmoil of day-to-day politics, more than a few thoughtful Americans have concluded that we are living a defining moment in our national life—roads are indeed diverging, and the choices taken will have much to do with whether the United States at its tercentenary in 2076 will be a political community in recognizable moral and cultural continuity with its founding.

As John Courtney Murray wrote in *We Hold These Truths*, in words that ring as true today as they did in 1960:

> What is at stake is America's understanding of itself. Self-understanding is the necessary condition of a sense of self-identity and self-confidence,

whether in the case of an individual or in the case of a people. If the American people can no longer base this sense on naive assumptions of self-evidence, it is imperative that they find other more reasoned grounds for their essential affirmation that they are uniquely a people, uniquely a free people. Otherwise the peril is great. The complete loss of one's identity is, with all propriety of theological definition, hell. In diminished forms it is insanity. And it would not be well for the American giant to go lumbering about the world today, lost and mad.

# The Handwriting on the Wall

## *Belshazzar, Daniel, Leo XIII, and Us*

During and after the Great Recession of the early twenty-first century, the phrase "the handwriting is on the wall" became a staple of the public conversation, a metaphor for the disorientation, unease, and fear for the future that seemed epidemic throughout the Western world and that had such a pronounced effect on electoral politics from Anchorage to Kyiv and virtually all points in between.

The phrase may have been ubiquitous, but how many of those who invoked "the handwriting on the wall" looked closely at its source, the fifth chapter of the Book of Daniel in the Old Testament? The story told there is a striking one. Recalling it in full might help us come to grips with whatever is being written on the wall at this moment in the history of the civilization of the West, and of the United States. Reflecting on that story might also help us identify a prophet who, like Daniel, could help us translate "the handwriting on the wall", understand its meaning, and thus know our duty.

The scene is readily set. The place: Babylon. The time: some two and a half millennia ago, in the sixth century B.C. The Kingdom of Judah has been conquered by the Chaldean king, Nebuchadnezzar, who, the Book of Daniel tells us, ordered his chief vizier "to bring some of the people of Israel, both of the royal family and of the nobility, youths without blemish, handsome and skilful in all wisdom, endowed with knowledge, understanding learning, and competent to serve in the king's palace, and to teach them the letters and language of the Chaldeans" (Dan 1:3–4). The most impressive of these talented young Jews was named Daniel. In addition to the personal qualities specified for royal service by Nebuchadnezzar, Daniel had the power to interpret the great king's dreams, a skill that led Nebuchadnezzar to acknowledge, for a moment at least, that Daniel's God, the God of the people of Israel, was "God of gods and Lord of kings, and a revealer of mysteries" (Dan 2:47).

Nebuchadnezzar's son, Belshazzar, was a man of a different character, however:

> King Belshazzar made a great feast for a thousand of his lords, and drank wine in front of the thousand. Belshazzar, when he tasted the wine, commanded that the vessels of gold and silver which Nebuchadnezzar his father had taken out of the temple in Jerusalem be brought, that the king and his lords, his wives, and his concubines might drink from them. Then they brought in the golden and silver vessels which had been taken out of the temple, the house of God in Jerusalem; and the king and his lords, his wives, and his concubines drank from them. They drank wine, and praised the gods of gold and silver, bronze, iron, wood, and stone.
>
> Immediately the fingers of a man's hand appeared and wrote on the plaster of the wall of the king's palace, opposite the lampstand; and the king saw the hand as it wrote. (Dan 5:1–5)

It was, we might imagine, an unwelcome interruption of the royal revels. Belshazzar, terrified, swore that he would make the man who could decipher the writing and its meaning the third ruler in the kingdom. The tenured academics and well-compensated op-ed writers of Belshazzar's dominions were stumped. Then the queen had an idea: call in Daniel. So the king summoned the Jewish exile and promised him the third position in the realm if he could read the handwriting on the wall and explain its meaning (Dan 5:13–16). The eponymous book tells the rest of the story:

> Then Daniel answered before the king: "Let your gifts be for yourself, and give your rewards to another; nevertheless I will read the writing to the king and make known to him the interpretation.... You have lifted up yourself against the Lord of heaven; and the vessels of his house have been brought in before you, and you and your lords, your wives, and your concubines have drunk wine from them; and you have praised the gods of silver and gold, of bronze, iron, wood, and stone, which do not see or hear or know, but the God in whose hand is your breath, and whose are all your ways, you have not honored.

"Then from his presence the hand was sent, and this writing was inscribed. And this was the writing that was inscribed: MENE, MENE, TEKEL, and PARSIN. This is the interpretation of the matter: MENE, God has numbered the days of your kingdom and brought it to an end; TEKEL, you have been weighed in the balances and found wanting; PERES, your kingdom is divided and given to the Medes and Persians."

Then Belshazzar commanded, and Daniel was clothed with purple, a chain of gold was put about his neck, and proclamation was made concerning him, that he should be the third ruler in the kingdom.

That very night Belshazzar the Chaldean king was slain. And Darius the Mede received the kingdom, being about sixty-two years old. (Dan 5:17, 23–31)

Belshazzar's feast and its denouement in the king's abrupt death is a biblical warning against the lethal effects of blasphemy—the worship of that which is not worthy of worship, which is the negation of worship. In his drunken arrogance, Belshazzar turned sacred vessels intended for true worship into playthings for debauchery, and because of that negation of worship, his claim to sovereignty was annulled. The handwriting on the wall spoke of this. And it spoke truly.

Is there similar handwriting on the wall in our own time? I think so. The words are different and they tend to be written, not telegraphically on walls by mysterious hands, but voluminously, in newspapers and magazines and books and scholarly journals and online. But these words, too, tell of the results of the negation of worship. Or, to put it in less dramatically biblical terms, the words on the wall at this moment in history speak of the results of a negation (a deconstruction) of the deep truths on which the civilization of the West, and the American democratic experiment, have been built. And one of the main things that the "handwriting on the wall" is telling us in the first decades of the twenty-first century is that the secular project is over.

By "secular project", I mean the effort, extending over the past two centuries or more, to erect an empty shrine at the heart of political modernity. This project's symbolic beginning may be dated precisely to April 4, 1791, when the French National Constituent Assembly ordered that the noble Parisian church of Saint Geneviève be transformed into a secular mausoleum, the Panthéon. The secular project accelerated throughout the nineteenth century as the high culture of Europe was shaped by what Henri de Lubac called "atheistic humanism": the claim, advanced by thinkers as diverse as Comte, Feuerbach, Marx, and Nietzsche, that the God of the Bible was the enemy of human maturity and must therefore be rejected in the name of human liberation. After atheistic humanism had produced, among other things, two world wars and the greatest slaughters in recorded history, a softer form of the "empty shrine" project emerged in the late twentieth century. This softer secularism—of which political science, not political philosophy, was the intellectual engine—focused on the institutional structures and processes of democracy and the market: if one got political structures and powers separated and balanced, and markets designed for maximum efficiency, then all one had to do was insert the key into the ignition and let politics and economics run by themselves.

In both its hard and soft forms, the secular project was wrong. Above all, it ignored the deep truth that it takes a certain kind of people, living certain virtues, to make democracy and the free economy work properly. People of that kind do not just happen. They must be formed in the habits of heart and mind, the *virtues*, that enable them to guide the machinery of free politics and free economics so that the net outcome is human flourishing, solidarity and civility, and the promotion of the common good. There is no such formation in the virtues of freedom available at the empty shrine.

A glimpse of what the empty shrine does produce was on offer in late summer 2011 in Great Britain, when packs of feral young people rampaged through city after city in an orgy of self-indulgence, theft, and destruction. The truth of what all that was about was most powerfully articulated by Lord Jonathan Sacks, the chief rabbi of the United Hebrew Congregations of the Commonwealth, writing in the *Wall Street Journal*:

> This was the bursting of a dam of potential trouble that had been building for years. The collapse of families and communities leaves in its wake unsocialized young people ... [who are the products of] a tsunami of wishful thinking that washed across the West, saying that you can have sex without the responsibility of marriage, children without the responsibility of parenthood, social order without

the responsibility of citizenship, liberty without the responsibility of morality, and self-esteem without the responsibility of work and earned achievement.

The inability of democratic countries to make rational decisions on education, social welfare, and health care in the face of potential fiscal disaster gives us another glimpse into the effects of the empty shrine and its inability to nurture and form men and women of democratic virtue—citizens capable of moral and economic responsibility in both their personal and public lives. Whether the venue is Athens or Madison, Wisconsin, the Piazza Venezia in Rome or McPherson Square in Washington, the underlying moral problem is the same: adults who have internalized a sense of entitlement that is wholly disconnected from a sense of responsibility. And once again, it was Rabbi Lord Sacks who connected the dots here when he wrote that the moral meltdown of the West—the attempt to build a civilization disconnected from the deep truths on which it was founded—had had inevitable economic and financial outcomes: "What has happened morally in the West is what has happened financially as well ... [as] people were persuaded that you could spend more than you earn, incur debt at unprecedented levels, and consume the world's resources without thinking about who will pay the bill and when." These linked phenomena—"spending our moral capital with the same reckless abandon that we have been spending our financial capital"—are, Sacks concluded, the inevitable result of a "culture of the free lunch in a world where there are no free lunches".

The gravest examples of the moral-cultural disease that is eating away at the vitals of the Western democracies may be found in places like Greece and Italy. There, public irrationality and political irresponsibility rendered the democratic system so dysfunctional that, under the pressure of the sovereign-debt crisis, the normal processes of democratic governance were temporarily replaced by the rule of technocratic elites, operating beneath a thin democratic veneer.

But Americans would be foolish if we did not see glimpses of the effects of the empty shrine in our own country. Those results come into view when we note the distinct absence of profiles in courage in our own politics; when entry into public service is essentially a projection of personal ego and self-esteem; when the crude exchange of epithets displaces serious engagement with the issues; when complexities are reduced to sound bites because the talk radio show must go on; when short-term political risk aversion leads to grave long-term consequences; when trans-generational solidarity is abandoned in the name of immediate gratification; when the question becomes what one can get out of the state (and its treasury), not, What am I contributing to the common good?

What these symptoms of democratic dysfunction suggest is that the empty shrine of the secularist project is not, in truth, entirely empty. For while it is true that the atheistic humanism of the nineteenth century and the democratic functionalism and economic libertarianism of the twentieth drained a lot of the moral energy from both free politics and free economics, the shrine at the heart of Western civilization has become the temple of a new form of worship: the worship of the imperial autonomous Self, which, in 1992, three justices of the U.S. Supreme Court famously promoted and celebrated as "the right to define one's own concept of existence, of meaning, of the universe, and of the mystery of human life".

That false worship of the Self—the adoration of that which is not worthy of adoration—has led to a severe attenuation of the moral sinews of democratic culture: the commitment to reason and truth-telling in debate; the courage to face hard facts squarely; the willingness to concede that others may have something to teach us; the ability to distinguish between prudent compromise and the abandonment of principle; the very idea of the common good, which may demand personal sacrifice.

If "the handwriting on the wall" is telling us that the secular project is over, then one of the lessons of that verdict can be put like this: while there are undoubtedly serious functional problems with Western institutions of governance in the early twenty-first century, the greatest deficit from which the Western democracies suffer today is a deficit, a hollowing-out, of democratic culture. And a primary cause of that deficit has been the profligate drawdown on the moral-cultural capital built up in the West under the influence of biblical religion.

What we call "the West" and the distinctive forms of political and economic life it has generated did not happen serendipitously. Moreover, those distinctive forms of politics and economics—democracy and the market—are not solely the product of the Continental European Enlightenment, a prominent misreading of modern history notwithstanding. The deeper taproots of our civilization lie in cultural soil nurtured by the fruitful and creative interaction of Jerusalem, Athens, and Rome: biblical religion, from which the West learned that history is a purposeful journey into the future, not just one damn thing after another; Greek rationality, which taught the West that there are truths embedded in the world and in us, and that we have access to those truths through the arts of reason; and Roman jurisprudence, which taught the West the superiority of the rule of law over the rule of brute force and raw coercion.

The three pillars of the West—Jerusalem, Athens, and Rome—are all essential, and they reinforce one another in a complex cultural dynamic. That mutual interdependence of Jerusalem, Athens, and Rome is another lesson that the handwriting on the wall in the early twenty-first century is teaching us. If, for example, you throw the God of the Bible over the side, as atheistic humanism demanded, you get two severe problems: one empirical, the other a matter of cultural temperament. Empirically, it seems that when the God of the Bible is abandoned in the name of human maturation and liberation, so is his first commandment, to "be fruitful and multiply" (Gen 1:28); and then one embarks on the kind of demographic winter that is central to the crisis of the European welfare state. Culturally, upon abandoning the God of the Bible, one begins to lose faith in reason. For as postmodernism has demonstrated, when reason is detached from belief in the God who imprinted the divine reason on the world—thus making creation intelligible through the Logos, the Word—reason soon turns in on itself. Then radical skepticism about the human capacity to know the truth of anything with clarity begets various forms of soured nihilism. And that lethal cocktail of skepticism and nihilism in turn yields moral relativism and the deterioration of the rule of law, as relativism is imposed on all of society by coercive state power.

Taking a cue from that great philosophical celebrant of irony, Richard Rorty, Colgate University's Robert Kraynak has neatly described the net result of all this as "freeloading atheism"—like Belshazzar's lords, wives, and concubines, those formed by the empty shrine and the worship of the imperial, autonomous Self have been drinking profligately out of sacred vessels, freeloading on moral truths that they do not acknowledge (and in many cases hold in contempt), but which are essential for sustaining democracy and the free economy, which the freeloaders claim to honor. But as Lord Sacks pointed out in 2011, that jig is up.

If the death of the secular project is one truth that "the handwriting on the wall" is teaching in our time, then so is the related death of postmodernism, which has been done in by the radical disconnect between "narrative" and reality. In recent years, the notion of "narrative" (which gave birth to that horrible neologism, "narrativizing") has become ubiquitous in the trans-Atlantic political vocabulary. To "change the narrative" is to gain political advantage; to "narrativize" a problem in a new way is taken as a way to solve it. Yet "changing the narrative" cannot change reality, and anchoring our public life to "narrative" rather than to reality can so warp our perceptions of reality that we end up like the White Queen in *Alice in Wonderland*, believing impossible things before breakfast—and lunch, and dinner.

This has become painfully obvious in Europe, where the public "narrative" of the post–World War II period, and particularly of the post–Cold War period, is the story of the creation of a community of social democracies living in harmony in a world beyond conflict. That narcotic and seductive "narrative" has crashed against reality, painfully. It has crashed against the consequences of an unprecedented reality in human history: systematic depopulation on a mass scale through deliberate, self-induced infertility. That infertility, in turn, set the stage for the twenty-first-century European fiscal crisis, the crisis of the modern European welfare state, and the immigration crisis. For the simple fact—the reality that no "narrative" can change—is that Europe does not have a sufficient number of taxpaying workers to sustain the social welfare states it has created. As if that were not bad enough, the post–Cold War European "narrative" has also crashed into the reality of spoiled and self-indulgent citizens whose productivity cannot deliver the standard of living that their politicians promise, those promises being yet another example of false "narratives".

The ability of a false "narrative" to warp our perception of reality is also evident in the claim that China will inevitably rise to become the dominant world power. This Sinophilia has a familiar Oriental ring to it. Twenty years ago, the leading candidate for the title of post–American hegemon was Japan, and an extended narrative of the inevitability of Japan's rise was spun out in best sellers like *Japan as Number One*. Today, however, Japan is living through an extended period of economic stagnation compounded by a demographic free fall that makes the very existence of the nation questionable over time. Now, the Asian contender for lead society in a post–American world is China. Yet that narrative, too, is crashing against demographic reality.

Thanks to its one-child policy, China will get old before it gets rich, with its population declining after 2020 and aging at a pace that will make it impossible to support growing cadres of retirees. Moreover, as Max Boot has written, "China must also deal with the fundamental illegitimacy of its unelected government, its lack of civil society, pervasive corruption, environmental devastation, and paucity of natural resources." These are facts; this is reality. Yet the "narrative" of China as the inevitable lead society of the future has become so familiar that the facts simply do not register beyond a small band of skeptics.

And then there is the damage that substituting "narrative" for reality has done in the United States: damage to the general health of the public discourse, and damage to our national security. From its early days, the Obama administration was so taken with the results of the "narrativizing" that worked wonders during the 2008 campaign that it imagined that "narrative" is the very point of government. As the president himself put it in an interview in the summer of 2011, reflecting on what he might have done differently, "the more you're in this office the more you have to say to yourself that telling a story to the American people is just as important as the actual policies that you're implementing." Presidents certainly must take seriously what the first President Bush dismissed, likely to his regret, as the "vision thing". But for a president to argue that what fundamentally matters in governance is story-telling bespeaks a mind awash in the intellectual exhaust fumes of postmodernism.

The difficulty, of course, is that ideas, even bad ideas, have consequences. The consequences of this commitment to "narrative" by the Obama administration certainly falsified domestic reality and made serious problem-solving far more difficult. They also put the nation, and the world, in greater jeopardy.

In foreign affairs, the equivalent of the Obama administration's commitment to changing narratives was the notion of a "new engagement", as if a change of declaratory policy and a less assertive (some would say more cringing) approach to difficult nations and difficult problems would change the problems themselves, perhaps even resolve them. It didn't.

After an American attempt at recasting the "narrative" with Russia and China in terms of "reengagement", both these veto-wielding members of the U.N. Security Council impeded efforts by the United States and others to constrain Iran's nuclear ambitions—ambitions that, if realized, would pose an existential threat to Israel (and perhaps several Arab countries) while creating a capacity for lethal terrorism on an unprecedented global scale.

After the Obama administration's "reset" with Russia (famously launched with a toy button that turned out to have the wrong Russian word engraved on it), Vladimir Putin's bullying (and worse) in the Russian "near abroad" intensified; authoritarianism increased within Russia itself; Russian efforts to pollute the global information space with disinformation became pandemic; and Russia provided support for such anti-American (and destabilizing) regimes as Bashar al-Assad's Syria and Hugo Chávez's Venezuela. "Resetting" with Russia—"changing the narrative"—also led to a betrayal of America's Polish and Czech allies on the question of missile defense and to a less-than-robust response to the Russian invasion and annexation of Crimea and a Russian-sponsored war in eastern Ukraine.

And then there was Iran. Here, the change of narrative began with an apology for American actions taken more than half a century ago, continued with negotiations that produced one American concession after another, and concluded with an agreement that virtually guaranteed that Iran will become a nuclear-weapons power. Moreover, the Iranian change-of-narrative game meant ignoring popular discontent with the Shiite mullahs' regime and effectively undercutting the possibility of the Iranian people shaking off the rule of the apocalyptic clerics and the Iranian Revolutionary Guard. Meanwhile, Iran continued to be a state sponsor of terrorism and, because of that, Americans were killed in Iraq and Afghanistan; Iran saber-rattled in the Strait of Hormuz; and Iran undertook assassination plots in Washington, D.C. And as it unfolded, this feckless attempt to change the "narrative" of America's dealings with Iran obscured from public view the reality of the situation, which is that regime change in Tehran is the only path to the reintegration of Iran into the community of responsible nations.

A change of "narrative" cannot change reality. But false narratives can so warp our perceptions of reality that matters are made worse. And matters made worse can, and often do, lead to matters made far more dangerous. That, too, is part of the twenty-first-century "handwriting on the wall".

In the fifth chapter of the Book of Daniel "the handwriting on the wall" bespoke the imminent demise of King Belshazzar's regime. I am not suggesting that "the handwriting on the wall" in the early twenty-first century bespeaks the inevitable demise of the West or of the United States. Like Rabbi Lord Sacks, I can look back in history on moments of social dissolution followed by rapid periods of cultural transformation and profound societal change. In his *Wall Street Journal* article, Sacks cited the rapid change of early industrial England under the influence of the Wesleyan revolution, which in two generations transformed British society in positive ways. Closer to our own time, we might recall the transformation of American culture, society, and law effected by the classic civil rights movement, another revolution of social change led by churchmen and built on the foundations of biblical faith. Then there was the nonviolent Revolution of 1989 in Central and Eastern Europe, which saw off European Communism after Pope John Paul II ignited a revolution of conscience in Poland that resonated throughout the Warsaw Pact with believers and unbelievers alike.

However, any such revolution in the twenty-first century will have to contend with social acids at least as corrosive as cheap gin in Dickensian London, institutionalized racism in America, and late bureaucratic socialism. It will have to contend with the intellectual detritus of the past two centuries, which has placed the imperial autonomous Self at the center of the Western civilizational project while reducing democracy and the free economy to matters of mechanics. Who is the Daniel who can read this "handwriting on the wall" and point a path, not to the demise of Western democracy, but to its moral and cultural renewal and thus its political transformation?

One possible candidate for that prophetic role is the Bishop of Rome who created the modern papacy, Pope Leo XIII. Born in 1810 into the minor Italian nobility and elected pope in 1878 as a caretaker, he died in 1903 after what was then the second-longest pontificate in reliably recorded history. Gioacchino Vincenzo Raffaele Luigi Pecci came to the papacy at one of the lowest points in that ancient office's historic fortunes. On the demise of the Papal States in 1870 and the pope's withdrawal from public view as the "prisoner of the Vatican", the great and good of Europe thought the papacy and the Church a spent force in world-historical terms. Yet over the next quarter-century, Leo XIII would prove to statesmen that he was, as Russell Hittinger put it, "the wiliest pope in centuries".

More to the point for our purposes, Leo XIII, as Professor Hittinger writes, was also possessed by "a relentless drive to diagnose historical contingencies in the light of first principles". He was, in that sense, a kind of papal public intellectual. Like his twentieth- and twenty-first-century papal successors, he, too, believed in reading "the signs of the times". But unlike the radical secularists of his time and ours, Leo XIII believed in reading the signs of the times through lenses ground by both faith and reason. His passion for understanding the deep currents of history through reason informed by a biblical vision of the human person and human communities is best remembered today for having launched the social doctrine of the Catholic Church. Yet Leo, who began to disentangle the Church in Europe from the evangelically stifling embrace of the old regimes, was also an acute analyst of the pathologies of political modernity. And it is that aspect of his thought and teaching that makes him a possible Daniel for our time, helping us read "the handwriting on the wall" as the freeloading pagans of modernity continue their carousing.

Leo's analysis of political modernity might be summarized in one phrase: no *telos*, no justice. Or, if you prefer: no metaphysics, no morals. Or, to leave the technical vocabulary of philosophy: no grounding of politics and economics in the deep truths of the human condition, no society fit for human beings.

The "empty shrine" at the center of political modernity was, for Leo XIII, the result of a dramatic revolution in European intellectual life in which metaphysics had been displaced from the center of reflection, thinking about thinking had replaced thinking about truth, and governance had therefore come unstuck from the first principles of justice. Science, which had replaced metaphysics as the most consequential of intellectual disciplines, could provide no answer to the moral question with which all politics, in the Western tradition, begins: How ought we to live together? Worse, when science stepped outside its disciplinary boundaries and tried its hand at social and political prescription, it let loose new demons, such as Social Darwinism, that would prove astonishingly lethal when they shaped the national tempers that made possible the great slaughters of the First World War.

Leo tried to fill the empty shrine at the heart of political modernity with reason, and with the moral truths that reason can discern. This was, to be sure, reason informed by biblical faith and Christian doctrine. But the genius of Leo XIII, public intellectual, was that he found a vocabulary to address the social, political, and economic problems of his time, and ours, that was genuinely ecumenical and accessible to all—the vocabulary of public reason, drawn from the natural moral law that is embedded in the world and in us. In one of his great encyclicals on political modernity, *Immortale Dei*, published in 1885, Leo wrote that "the best parent and guardian of liberty amongst men is truth." Unlike the postmodern Pontius Pilates who imagine that the cynical question "What is truth?" ends the argument, Leo XIII understood that this question, which can be asked in a noncynical and genuinely inquiring way, is the beginning of any serious wrestling with the further question, "How ought we to live together?"

This general orientation to the problem of political modernity then led Leo to pose a cultural challenge to the post–ancien régime public life of the West: a challenge to think more deeply about law, about the nature of freedom, about civil society and its relationship to the state, and about the limits of state power.

Leo XIII's concept of law, drawn from Thomas Aquinas, challenged the legal positivism of his time and ours, according to which the law is what the law says it is, period. That may be true, at a very crude level. But such positivism (which is also shaped by the modern tendency to see civil laws as analogous to the "laws" of nature) empties law of moral content, detaches it from reason, and treats it as a mere expression of human willfulness. Leo challenged political modernity to a nobler concept of law, synthesized by Russell

Hittinger as "a binding precept of reason, promulgated by a competent authority for the common good". Thus law is not mere coercion; law is authoritative *prescription* grounded in reason. True law reflects moral judgment, and its power comes from its moral persuasiveness. Law appeals to conscience, not just to fear.

Given this understanding of law, it should come as no surprise that Leo challenged political modernity to a nobler concept of freedom. Following Thomas Aquinas rather than William of Ockham (the first proto-modern distorter of the truth about freedom), Leo XIII insisted that freedom is not sheer willfulness. Rather, as Leo's successor John Paul II would later put it, freedom is the human capacity to know what is truly good, to choose it freely, and to do so as a matter of habit, or virtue. According to this line of argument, a talent for freedom grows in us; we cut short that learning process if we insist, with the culture of the imperial autonomous Self, that my freedom consists in doing what I want to do, *now*.

Leo XIII's challenge to political modernity was also a challenge to the omnicompetence of the state. Leo was a committed defender of what we would call "civil society", or what were called "voluntary private associations" in his day. Political community, according to Leo XIII, was composed of a richly textured pluralism of associations, some natural and some more contingent, of which the state was but one (albeit an important one). These associations (which, to reduce the matter to its simplest form, included everything from the family to business and labor associations to civic groups and religious communities) were not merely barriers against the reach of state power; they were goods in themselves, communities expressing different forms of friendship and solidarity. Thus the just state would take care to protect these societies (akin to Edmond Burke's "small platoons"), which contributed to the common good in unique ways—and not least by forming the habits of heart and mind that made willful men and women, constantly tempted to selfishness, into good citizens.

Moreover, Leo proposed, the state's responsibility to provide legal protection for the functioning of natural and voluntary associations ought not to be something conceded out of a sense of largesse or governmental noblesse oblige. That responsibility, too, was a matter of first principles—in this case, the principle of the limited, law-governed state. For the state that can recognize natural and voluntary associations that exist prior to the state, not just as a matter of historical chronology but as a matter of the deep truths of the human condition, is a state that has recognized the boundary markers of its own competence, and thus the limits of its legitimate reach.

In the first papal social encyclical, *Rerum Novarum*, published in 1891, Leo XIII wrote presciently about many of the debates of our own time; he also anticipated the disputes animating contemporary arguments as seemingly diverse as the definition of marriage, the reach of the Equal Employment Opportunity Commission, and the regulatory powers of the U.S. Department of Health and Human Services. The specific form of voluntary association addressed in *Rerum Novarum* was the trade union, but the principle Leo articulated applies throughout the rich associational matrix of civil society: "The State should watch over these societies of citizens banded together in accordance with their rights, but it should not thrust itself into their peculiar concerns and their organization, for things move and live by the spirit inspiring them, and may be killed by the rough grasp of a hand from without."

In the first quarter of the twenty-first century, the American people are confronted with a full menu of mega-questions. Will the United States continue to "lead from behind" in world affairs, as the Obama administration described its strategy? Will the United States succumb to the siren songs of "America First"? Or will America resume its place as the indispensable country "at the point" in confronting threats to world order?

Will the United States follow the social model pioneered by post–World War II Western Europe, or will it devise new ways of combining compassion, justice, personal responsibility, and public fiscal discipline?

Can the challenges of globalization be met in ways that expand, rather than diminish, the middle class?

Will the federal judiciary continue to provide legal ballast for the doomed secular project, or will it permit the normal mechanisms of democratic self-governance to advance a nobler understanding of freedom, and indeed of law itself?

Will religious freedom remain the first liberty of these United States, or will religious communities be pushed farther to the margins of public life?

Will the legal architecture of America promote a culture of life or a culture of death?

These are all questions of grave import. On first glance they can appear like a broken kaleidoscope that never resolves itself into discernible patterns and connections. Or, to return to that now-familiar biblical image, "the handwriting on the wall" can seem indecipherable. Yet with Leo XIII's acute analysis of political modernity as our guide, perhaps we can decipher the writing and discern its meaning. "The handwriting on the wall" at this moment in history is telling us that a political culture detached from the deep truths embedded in the human condition eventually strengthens and emboldens traits of selfishness and irresponsibility that ill-befit citizens of a democracy. "The handwriting on the wall" is telling us that a democratic politics that ignores those deep truths eventually dissolves into thinly disguised dictatorship: the dictatorship of relativism. And if that is the message, then our duty comes into clearer focus, too.

If the rule of law, the heritage of Rome, is threatened among us, not just by demagogy, rioting and enraged protesters, and unfocused fear, but by the transformation of law into coercion in the name of misguided compassion, then we should look to Jerusalem and Athens—to a revival of the biblical image of mankind's origin and destiny and to a rediscovery of the arts of reason—as the means by which to rebuild the foundations of democracy. In Psalm 11:3, the biblical poet asks what those who care for justice are to do "if the foundations are destroyed". The beginning of an answer to that poignant question is to disentangle ourselves from the notion that the ratchet of history works in only one direction.

Then, having regained a sense of possibility about the present and purposefulness about the future, we can proceed to rebuild the foundations of the political culture of the United States, and of the West, through a deepening of biblical faith and a reassertion of the prerogatives of reason in the name of a noble concept of law-governed democracy.

# The Importance of Reality Contact

## *Deep Truths and Public Policy*

The glossary of inadmissible words in twenty-first-century American society has shrunk to what seems, at times, a null set. Deprecations, sexual innuendos, and excretory references that once got kids' mouths washed out with soap are dropped with aplomb and immunity—and in presidential debates, not just Quentin Tarantino films. On the rare occasions when the Federal Communications Commission chastises a broadcaster for letting an expletive pass uncensored or unbleeped, cries of repression ricochet from sea to shining sea, quickly followed by passionate defenses of the First Amendment.

But the set of inadmissible words is not quite null just yet. For, to paraphrase Saint Paul in the thirteenth chapter of First Corinthians, there still abideth metaphysics. Indeed, twenty-first-century postmodern culture does not simply shun the *word* "metaphysics". It dismisses out of hand the very notion that there is a morally significant givenness to reality: a structure of The Way Things Are that can be discerned by reason and that, being known, discloses certain truths about the way we should live. In twenty-first-century America, and throughout the twenty-first-century West, what the American Founders would have called "the pursuit of happiness" has become a function of the autonomous will of the individual, and that willfulness can legitimately attach itself to any object so long as no one gets hurt.

The drastic attenuation of these three great ideas—that there are deep truths built into the world, into human beings, and into human relationships; that these truths can be known by reason; and that knowledge of these truths is essential to living virtuously, which means living happily—has taken place over a very long period of time. A good argument can be made that one of the prime villains of the piece was the fourteenth-century philosopher William of Ockham, whose voluntarism shifted the locus of Western moral reflection from the intellect (which was to discover moral truths in reality) to the will (which could impose, or even invent, its own moral reality). The wedge that the eighteenth-century Scottish Enlightenment philosopher David Hume tried to drive between "is" and "ought", which accelerated Western philosophy's lurch into subjectivism, was surely part of the problem, as was the failure of Immanuel Kant's "categorical imperative" to meet Hume's challenge and reground moral reflection and judgment in something other than the inside of our heads. Twentieth-century analytical philosophies that reduced thought about the human condition to a variety of language games didn't help matters either.

But even if the philosophers got caught in what Polish thinker Wojciech Chudy once called the "trap of reflection", what about the impact of reality itself? One might have thought that the mass slaughters perpetrated by the mid-twentieth-century totalitarianisms would have compelled a general cultural revulsion against a will to power unchecked by ideas of true and false, good and evil. Yet even those experiences of awfulness don't seem to have bent the curve of cultural history away from self-absorption and willfulness, as that cultural history is manifest in the world of ideas.

Perhaps it should not have been surprising that American higher education shifted gears rather readily from John Dewey to Jacques Derrida: from the anorexic philosophy of pragmatism to a postmodern insouciance about (and indeed hostility to) any notion of deep truths embedded in the world and in us. The native-born American professoriate hadn't been scarred by the experience of gulags and extermination camps; and in any event American higher education, largely dissenting-Protestant in origin, had never been securely grounded in the classic verities of the metaphysical sensibility that grew out of Aristotle as mediated by Catholic medieval thinkers like Thomas Aquinas.

What is surprising, though—and what ought to be disturbing, if illuminating—is the rapidity with which university life behind the old Iron Curtain turned on a dime from Marxism to postmodernism in the aftermath of the Cold War. It took the University of California at Berkeley a full century to become *Berkeley*. It took the venerable Jagiellonian University in Kraków (founded in 1364) less than a decade to become a Central European simulacrum of Berkeley in its fascination with postmodern canons of epistemological skepticism, moral relativism, and metaphysical nihilism. That blink-of-an-eye transformation suggests that there is a deep cultural turbulence beneath the surface of Western civilization in this second decade of the twenty-first century. To describe it in the terms above, however, is not to suggest that this disturbance is a problem for philosophers only. Quite the contrary.

That Western democratic bodies ranging from the Greek Parliament to the Italian Chamber of Deputies to the United States Congress and the California State Assembly find it impossible to craft and adopt public policies that meet the pressing demands of the moment (while frittering away their time in various forms of political theater) suggests that the deterioration of Western thought about Things As They Are has had dramatic public-policy consequences—and could eventually have the gravest civilizational consequences. That the politics of the Western democracies are often in gridlock is not simply because there are deeply different views of personal freedom and public goods in competition in public life; that has always been the case. The difference today is that there are no agreed-upon, reality-based reference points to which the contending parties can appeal in order to settle the argument about the public good and how it ought to be achieved.

Public policy that fosters individual human flourishing and the common good must take account of reality, and realities. When a culture loses confidence in its capacity to say, with conviction, "This is The Way Things Are", its capacity to devise ways and means of addressing The Way Things Ought To Be is severely eroded. In a culture without metaphysics, the one trump card in public life becomes individual willfulness. And then, because politics is an expression of culture, both the citizenry and its political leaders increasingly come to resemble exiles in a wilderness of mirrors, beset by myopia and astigmatism and incapable of seeing anything other than each individual's bundle of desires—desires that become the only meaningful unit-of-account in politics.

Reality contact, it seems, is important not only for personal mental health. Reality contact is essential to making democracy work. Yet an insistence on avoiding reality is more or less the organizing principle of our contemporary political life. It lies at the center of a great many of our public problems, and it connects them to one another.

The desire to separate those problems and handle them individually—say, to "put aside the social issues" and just worry about tax reform, as many an adviser to the twenty-first-century Republican Party suggests—is no less naïve and unreal an approach to political life than is the desire to ignore the substance of each problem and pretend we can inhabit a world of our own imagination. Responsible, democratic self-governance, and effective public policy that addresses rather than postpones problems, begins by accepting reality. That this seems awfully difficult for many of our fellow citizens these days is perhaps the most grave of our problems.

There is another, parallel, way to think about these deeper cultural currents that are helping make it extremely difficult for even serious political leaders (with which the West is not exactly replete in the twenty-first century) to connect the dots between, say, certain public goods (financial security for increasingly elderly populations and quality medical care for all) and certain fiscal realities (this is how much money we can raise through taxation without destroying economic initiative, and this is how much we can responsibly borrow). And that is to understand that, for the past half-century or so, the United States and the rest of the West have been living through an intense Gnostic revival—a powerful recrudescence of an ancient heresy that has erupted time and again over the past two millennia and that is very much with us today.

Gnosticism is a protean cultural virus that has taken many forms over two millennia. Wherever and whenever it has appeared, however, Gnosticism has sought the good *outside* of reality as we perceive it through the materials of this world. In the Gnostic view, human flourishing (to use a contemporary term) comes from the possession of a *gnosis*, a knowledge, that will lift men and women out of the grubbiness of the quotidian and into the purified realm of truth. Reality, in the Gnostic view, is antithetical to "the pursuit of happiness"; reality is to be rejected, and thereby overcome.

Contemporary Gnosticism, which is most powerfully embodied in the sexual revolution, has given all this a new twist by masking its essential deprecation of The Way Things Are by what appears, at first blush, to be a hypermaterialism: a cult of sensuality *über alles* in which sexual gratification, in any form among consenting adults, is the highest of goods and the most inalienable of personal liberties. But the deeper dimension of the new Gnosticism, especially as it manifests itself through the sexual revolution, is the conviction that there are no Things As They Are. None. *Everything* in the human condition is plastic and malleable. Everything can (and ought to be allowed to) be bent to human willfulness, which is to say, to human desire. As for the notion that some desires are untoward, even wicked, because they lead to self-degradation and thus frustrate the natural quest for happiness—well, if there are no Things As They Are, how can anyone say that this desire or that is unnatural, dehumanizing, or wrong?

In this respect, the most powerful expression of the ancient cultural toxin of Gnosticism in the twenty-first-century West is the ideology of gender—the body of thought that quite naturally occupied the cultural vacuum left when metaphysics and any sense of reality-grounded thinking about the human condition collapsed, when technology made it possible to sunder sex from procreation readily, privately, and inexpensively, and when the law built a high wall of protection around sexual encounters between consenting adults. The sexual revolution imagined itself, at the outset, to be liberating men and women from hoary religious constraints and their attendant psychological catarrhs. Yet the cultural transformation that the sexual revolution unleashed would turn out to have far more profound consequences than those imagined by its early propagandists, who seem to have imagined sex as just another contact sport.

For within a very short span of time, less than two generations, two aspects of the human condition that had been understood for millennia to be the very quintessence of *givenness*—maleness and femaleness—were no longer taken to be given at all. "Male" and "female" were *not* The Way Things Are. "Male" and "female" were "cultural constructs", usually manipulated by those in power for purposes of domination (Gnosticism thus adding a *frisson* of revolutionary Marxism to its ideology of plasticity).

The beginnings of this path of radical, Gnostic cultural transformation may have been marked by *Playboy* and the pill. Where it was all heading became clear when Spain's Zapatero government enacted, in 2007, legislation allowing men to change themselves into women (and vice versa) by a simple declaration at a Civil Registry office (and without any surgical folderol)—after which affirmation a new national identity card, noting the new gender, would be issued. It is hard to imagine a more explicit expression of personal willfulness overpowering natural givenness. (As I noted at the time, with more frivolity than the situation warranted, the most famous line in *My Fair Lady* would have to be changed so that it now read, "The dame in Spain/is mainly in the name.")

Gnostic anthropology—the Gnostic view of the human person and the human condition—is the antithesis of the biblical view of men and women and their possibilities, which has long been one of the foundation stones of the Western civilizational project. Thus it was no accident, although it seemed to many a happy and perhaps strategically important cultural development, that when the premier intellectual in early twenty-first-century Christianity took up the cudgels against the radical cultural transformation wrought by the new Gnosticism and raised a warning flag about its public implications, he cited the anti-Gnostic critique of the ideology of gender by a prominent Jewish leader.

As French president François Hollande pressed a same-sex marriage bill in the National Assembly in the fall of 2012, the chief rabbi of France, Gilles Bernheim, offered the French government a detailed critique of Hollande's proposal in a twenty-five-page essay that caught the attention of Pope Benedict XVI. Then, when Benedict gave his annual Christmas address to the senior officials of the Roman Curia on December 21, 2012, he noted the dramatic decline of the marriage culture of the West, warned that this presaged a social world in which "man remains closed in on himself and keeps his 'I' ultimately for himself, without really rising above it", and then buttressed his argument by adopting Rabbi Bernheim's critique as a summary of the countercase to the Gnostic gender revolution.

"While up to now we regarded a false understanding of the nature of human freedom as one cause of the crisis of the family," Benedict told his audience, "it is now becoming clear that the very notion of being—of what being human really means—is being called into question." He continued:

[Rabbi Bernheim] quotes the famous saying of Simone de Beauvoir: "One is not born a woman, one becomes so" (*On ne naît pas femme, on le devient*). These words lay the foundation for what is put forward today under the term "gender" as a new philosophy of sexuality. According to this philosophy, sex is no longer a given element of nature that man has to accept and personally make sense of: it is a social role that we choose for ourselves, while in the past it was chosen for us by society. The profound falsehood of this theory and of the anthropological revolution contained within it is obvious. People dispute the idea that they have a nature, given by their bodily identity, that serves as a defining element of the human being. They deny their nature and decide that it is not something previously given to them, but that they make it for themselves. According to the biblical creation account, being created by God as male and female pertains to the essence of the human creature. This duality is an essential aspect of what being human is all about, as ordained by God. This very duality as something previously given is what is now disputed. The words of the creation account: "male and female he created them" (Gen 1:27) no longer apply. No, what now applies is this: it was not God who created them male and female—hitherto society did this, now we decide for ourselves. Man and woman as created realities, as the nature of the human being, no longer exist. Man calls his nature into question. From now on he is merely spirit and will.

To imagine that we live in such a self-created world is not only to imagine that we owe nothing to our given nature but also to believe that we owe no attention or response to the problems that arise when we ignore that nature. Such a warped sensibility not only makes any moral order impossible; it makes political order untenable, too.

Some who share the concerns of Pope Benedict and Rabbi Bernheim will nonetheless suggest that these are essentially matters of the private sphere, with little discernible consequence for public policy and public life beyond some adjustments to civil marriage law. Others, perhaps also sympathetic to Benedict and Bernheim in theory or sentiment, will sigh and argue that the debate has been lost, that the sexual revolution has won, and that arguments about public policy on issues ranging from tax reform to entitlement reform to health care to foreign policy must now be conducted on their own merits, absent the distractions of these fevered questions of sex, gender, and so forth. This idea that the "social issues" can be put aside so that other issues can be taken up has been frequently championed as the prudent course for American conservatives and for the Republican Party.

Yet if politics really is an expression of culture (as political theory is an extension of ethics), then the Gnostic revolution and the decline of cultural confidence in The Way Things Are must be, in fact, at the very center of our politics. A people convinced that all is plastic and malleable in the human condition—that nothing simply *is*, even when it comes to such seemingly elementary givens as maleness and femaleness and their natural complementarity—is going to perceive politics in a distinctive, and likely distorting, way. For even those who have never heard of Gnosticism, much less imagined themselves as its adherents, are nonetheless going to think in Gnostic categories.

The most obvious example of this is the course taken by the "same-sex marriage" debate. Now, to be sure, the Human Rights Campaign and other "same-sex marriage" advocates were quite shrewd in battening on the American civil rights movement as the icon of their own activism and in not publicly pressing that activism toward its logical conclusion (which is the legalization of polygamy and polyandry, already being bruited in elite law journals). But these shrewd political tactics worked because the political culture had been previously softened up (and dumbed down) by the new Gnostic revolution.

Thus a patently false analogy—legal recognition of marriage as a union between a man and a woman, period, was exactly the same as the anti-miscegenation laws that proscribed marriage between blacks and whites in the era of racial segregation—was successfully sold because a culture resistant to the idea that some realities just *are* will easily swallow the rhetorical bait. Such a culture is then utterly befuddled when the most intellectually sophisticated Catholic bishop in American history, Francis Cardinal George of Chicago, wrote in his archdiocesan newspaper that Illinois' proposed same-sex marriage legislation "is less a threat to religion than it is an affront to human reason and the common good of society. It means that we all are to pretend to accept something we know is physically impossible. The Legislature might just as well repeal the law of gravity."

But the new Gnosticism warps our politics in other ways that ought to concern those thinkers, commentators, and politicians now

counseling their fellow conservatives to admit that the sexual revolution has triumphed, to get over it, and to move on. For that counsel
prompts an urgent question: Move on *how*? If people are prepared to
believe (or, even worse, if people are prepared to insist as a matter of
fundamental civil rights) the unreal claim that marriage can encompass two men or two women, why should those same people not
believe that America can continue to run trillion-dollar deficits with
impunity? Or that the centralization and vast regulatory apparatus
created by Obamacare will not inevitably lead to the rationing of
end-of-life care? Or that the federal budget deficit has primarily to do
with the wealthy not paying "their fair share"?

Every serious analyst of the impending federal fiscal crisis, from the
right and the left alike, understands that there are very hard choices
to be made in building an American future that combines financial
responsibility with justice and compassion. But how can such difficult
choices and policies be sold, on the basis of the realities that are self-
evidently clear from the numbers, to a population culturally condi-
tioned to think that nothing is as is, that everything is malleable and
plastic? Why, for example, should a population that thinks of children
primarily as a lifestyle choice aimed at enhancing parental satisfaction
take seriously the grave moral problem of saddling future generations
(as well as current ones) with unpayable, and perhaps even unservice-
able, amounts of public debt?

Foreign policy is also imperiled by the new Gnosticism and its
reality-denying effects on personal and public perceptions. Putting
aside the question of whether the World War II generation was the
greatest American generation—what about the Founders?—surely
the greatness of the generation that fought and beat Nazism and Japanese imperialism was that it accepted the duty to do just that as an
imperative imposed by reality. Throughout World War II, there was
very little of the flag-waving, chest-thumping, martial romanticism
that had characterized the American entry into the First World War.
As William Manchester, Paul Fussell, and others have observed, Americans approached the Second World War as a dirty, necessary job that
had to be done, period. When given serious political leadership by
reality-grounded men like Harry Truman and Dwight Eisenhower,
that same generation understood that more sacrifices were required to
fight what John F. Kennedy in his inaugural address called "the long
twilight struggle" against another totalitarian threat. But today?

If twenty-first-century Americans perceive the world through cultural lenses distorted by Gnosticism, how can we think strategically and wisely about the normality of conflict in international affairs? How can we grasp that foreign policy is a matter of crafting incentives and disincentives to get others to behave as we would like them to behave? How can a people accustomed to thinking of the world as fungible and elastic possibly comprehend the threat posed by religiously inspired apocalyptics whose idea of changing the world is to end the world as we know it? The link between the new Gnosticism and foreign policy "resets" or "America First" fantasies may not be immediately evident, but the dots are there, and those dots can be connected if "resetting" reality itself has become a deeply ingrained (and publicly celebrated) cultural habit.

America tried a flight from harsh international realities in the 1990s during the Clinton administration, which was the first significant embodiment of the Gnostic temperament in the history of the presidency. The result was the chaotic, ghastly, and still unresolved dissolution of Yugoslavia, the refusal to see reality for what it was in the Rwandan genocide, the scuttle from Somalia, the naïveté of "Oslo" as the magic solution to the Middle East's problems, the bombings of our embassies in Kenya and Tanzania, the attack of the U.S.S. *Cole*—and, ultimately, 9/11.

That same flight from reality, shaped in part by the same Gnosticism (filtered in this instance through certain New Left confusions), led during President Obama's term of office to a revival of Russian power and a new Russian aggressiveness east of the old Iron Curtain. It produced the betrayal of American allies like Poland and the Czech Republic, the expulsion of American pro-democracy groups from both the Middle East and Russia, the Russian annexation of Crimea and an ongoing Russian-backed war in eastern Ukraine, continued Iranian pursuit of nuclear weapons, and no discernible change of perspective among the Palestinian political leadership. Ultimately, this unwillingness to accept Things As They Are brought about the murder of a U.S. ambassador and American diplomatic staff in Benghazi.

Reality may be, and often is, unpleasant. But policies rooted in a failure to grasp reality are dangerous, and too often deadly. Those conservatives who imagine that there is no linkage between the unreality embodied in the sexual revolution and the ideology of gender, and the unreality embodied in the fiscal, health-care, social-welfare, and foreign policies they oppose, might well think again. A culture convinced that everything is malleable and that there are no givens in personal or public life is not a culture likely to sustain serious debates about serious public-policy options. Those who find such debates lacking in American public life today—which is to say, anyone paying serious attention—had best start thinking about the deeper roots of the problem that lie in the loss of a cultural grip on Things As They Are.

In 2006, the distinguished French philosopher and historian of ideas Rémi Brague made a suggestive proposal for periodizing modern Western political history, which I've noted before but which is worth revisiting in this context. The nineteenth century, he argued, was a period focused on good and evil. The "social question"—prompted by the Industrial Revolution, urbanization, mass education, and the demise of traditional society—shaped the public landscape.

The twentieth century had been the century of true or false. Built on the foundations of desperately wrongheaded ideas of human beings, their origins, communities, and destiny, totalitarian ideologies defined the contest for the human future that drove history from the aftermath of World War I (the event that began "the twentieth century" as an epoch) through the Soviet crack-up of 1991 (the event that ended "the twentieth century" as a distinctive political-historical period).

And the twenty-first century? That, Brague proposed, would be the century of being and nothingness: the epoch of the metaphysical question. This might seem, in comparison to Brague's descriptions of the nineteenth and twentieth centuries, a rather abstract notion. Yet Brague, in his French way, was being very practical and concrete in defining our times in those terms. For if there is nothing received and cherished by our culture that might be called the "grammar of the human"—if there are no Things As They Are—then everything is up for grabs, cacophony drowns out intelligent public debate, and politics is merely the will to power.

Having spent decades immersed in the study of Islamic philosophy and law, Rémi Brague was hardly unaware of the threat posed to the West by jihadism, both externally and internally. But he insisted that there was a prior "enemy within the gates" of our own making.

It was nihilism, a kind of soured cynicism about the very mystery of being and its goodness. Such cynicism drains life of meaning, fore-shortens horizons of expectation, and renders sacrifices for the common good risible.

Brague found it foreshadowed in the Enlightenment intellectual (left unnamed) who once said that he did not have children because begetting children was a criminal act, a matter of condemning another human being to death. A similar nihilism may be found at the root of today's diminishing marriage culture, in the treatment of children as lifestyle accessories, in the trivialization of sexuality in advertising and entertainment, and in so many other expressions of the Gnostic ideology of gender and the sexual revolution.

The question, then, is being. Serious thought about the political future of the Western democracies will not end, or perhaps even begin, with metaphysics. But serious reflection on the future of America and the West cannot ignore the grammar of the human, because that reflection cannot address what ails us, our politics, and our civilization without first accepting the reality of Things As They Are.

# A New Great Awakening

## *The Gregorian Option for American Cultural Reform*

In the late 1980s, Richard John Neuhaus announced a project with a large ambition: to develop a "religiously-public philosophy for the American experiment in ordered liberty". Drawing on the truths of biblical religion and the rich patrimony of Western political theory, the goal was to craft a moral-cultural compass by which the nation might steer a virtuous path through the twenty-first century, following the victory of imperfect democracies over pluperfect tyrannies in the Cold War.

In October 2016, Australian political commentator Paul Kelly suggested that the hope of achieving that goal had been dealt a hard, and possibly lethal, blow by the 2016 election campaign. "Only a fool could miss the global significance of this election," Kelly wrote.

> It is a massive advertisement for American weakness, not weakness in a quantified way but weakness at the nation's heart, rottenness at its core. Since its formation America, despite its grievous faults, has endured as a "city upon a hill"—invoking the Puritan vernacular—an example to the world as extolled by both John F. Kennedy and Ronald Reagan. This election, by contrast, is a display of American ugliness, vulgarity, and selfishness. What nation will want to duplicate the American rule book after this event? What nation would want to follow American democracy?

And that's a friend of the United States talking. We may only imagine what others were thinking, both those who wish to see the United States cut down to size and those who wish its demise, period.

Serious criticism of American political culture, however, has been homegrown as well as imported. For since the unparalleled raucousness before and after Election Day 2016, Americans of all political persuasions have been asking themselves two questions: "What *happened*? And *now* what?" There is, of course, no lack of either diagnosis or prescription.

According to some analysts, 2016 tore the soiled dressings off a festering wound and unmasked the now-undeniable fact that America has become two nations. Some describe the divide as one between cultural traditionalists and cultural progressives; others between the economically empowered and the economically disempowered; still others between the responsible and the irresponsible. Not a few commentators think that permanent estrangement across these divides is more likely in the contemporary United States than fluidity and mobility—not to mention civility, comity, and solidarity.

Others dug a bit deeper into the substrata of our public life, trying to parse what 2016 revealed and what might be done about it. Political philosopher and intellectual historian George Nash cautioned against the rise of something never before seen in American history: an "ideologically muddled, 'nationalist-populist' major party combining both leftwing and rightwing elements". National security analyst Thomas Donnelly noted a disturbing similarity between the two castes that inhabit Charles Murray's paradigmatic American locales, "Belmont" and "Fishtown"—both the beneficiaries of a globalized economy in "Belmont" and those in "Fishtown" who think themselves its victims "measure their lives in material terms", which is a far cry from the Republic of Virtue imagined by, say, John Quincy Adams. Dominican theologian Thomas Joseph White made a similar point in a different key when he wrote, just before the election, that "postmodernity is an era of spiritual impoverishment and metaphysical pessimism", both of which warp even the noblest of human desires.

The prescriptions have also run the gamut, from those that deal with surface manifestations of our national discontent, to those proposing structural changes in our government, to those addressing deeper issues.

The weekend before the 2016 election, the "Saturday Essay" in the *Wall Street Journal*, written by two social psychologists, proposed that a "truce" for America's "tribal politics" might be achieved if everyone would try to speak civilly to someone with whom they disagreed—a prescription unlikely to yield immediate success, given that the cacophony in our national life became even worse approximately ninety-six hours after the essay first appeared. Ten days after the electorate declared itself, Peggy Noonan suggested that "maybe things can be soothed" if "the cultural left eases up and the economic right loosens up," another well-intended suggestion, and one that might have worked in a less turbulent time. But it was immediately rendered moot by numerous demonstrations that the cultural left thinks the ratchet of history turns in only one direction and is prepared to be violently disruptive to underscore that conviction.

Former Florida governor Jeb Bush, for his part, recognized that something dramatic had emerged in American public life during the primary elections in which his candidacy was overwhelmed by a tsunami of discontent: an "anger and deep distrust ... toward Washington", as he put it, by voters who "believe the American dream is increasingly out of reach" because they believe "our system is skewed in favor of the powerful and the connected." His prescription? Bush proposed a constitutional convention to "pass [congressional] term limits, a balanced-budget amendment, and restraints on the Commerce Clause, which has given the federal government far more regulatory power than the Founders intended."

There are elements of truth to be found in all of these analyses, and several of the prescriptions are worth serious attention. The country has indeed become bifurcated along fault lines that now seem more like chasms than temporary cracks in the façade of our national life. There is something ominously reminiscent of Europe in the 1920s and 1930s in the xenophobic nationalism and statism evident in some expressions of the new American populism. Both prosperity and stagnation—decadence, and what J.D. Vance has dubbed "learned helplessness"—are eroding the American spirit. The communitarian ethos that long distinguished the United States has clearly frayed, and not just at the edges. And does anyone really doubt that we are less noble a people as the worship of the God of the Bible has been displaced in many quarters by the worship of the imperial autonomous Self?

All of that can and should be conceded and faced squarely. Still, an answer to the two questions so many have been asking—What *happened*? *Now* what?—may become clearer when we drill down into the subsoil from which the present discontents have emerged. This effort must begin with three steps.

The first step is to recognize that American political culture is in crisis because our public moral culture is in crisis. The second step is to recognize that American public moral culture is in crisis because of a false understanding of freedom. And the third step is to recognize that the false notion of freedom evident across the spectrum of American politics—although perhaps most obviously on the political-cultural left—is based on a false anthropology: a distorted idea of the human person and human aspirations.

This analytic approach assumes, of course, that democracies like the American republic are not machines that can run by themselves; democracy is not a hardware that can be run by any software. Rather, the machinery of democracy—constitutionally protected and enumerated rights, separation of powers, a robust interaction between the executive and legislative branches of government, an independent judiciary, and a free press that functions as a public ombudsman according to professional standards of probity and fairness—only works when that machinery rests on a firm moral-cultural foundation. Or to put it another way, the machinery of democratic self-governance works only when a critical mass of citizens are internally self-governing and live their lives against a horizon of aspiration that extends beyond their own pleasures and financial aggrandizement.

With thinkers ranging from Thomas Jefferson to Václav Havel to John Paul II, I take it that an aspiration to freedom is built into the human condition. We are, as it were, hardwired for freedom. But that aspiration must be mediated through a true culture of freedom, if the aspiration is to become publicly embodied in a national capacity for self-governance that leads to genuine human flourishing.

Or, to vary James Carville's dictum during the 1992 presidential election, "It's the culture, stupid." And it is at that level that we can begin to understand and address the national crisis of political culture that 2016 revealed.

To begin with diagnosis, where do we find the implicit anthropology—the vision of the human person and the tacit definition of noble human aspiration—that underwrites American public life today?

While its roots go back to the High Middle Ages and the concept of freedom-as-willfulness proposed by William of Ockham, a more recent iteration of it may be found in the 1992 Supreme Court decision *Planned Parenthood of Southeastern Pennsylvania v. Casey*. There, as previously noted, the Court plurality composed of Justices Anthony Kennedy, Sandra Day O'Connor, and David Souter grounded their reaffirmation of a liberty right to abortion on demand in a distinctive concept of freedom. "At the heart of liberty," the justices famously wrote, "is the right to define one's own concept of existence, of meaning, of the universe, and of the mystery of human life." Twenty-three years later, writing for the Court's 5–4 majority in *Obergefell v. Hodges*, the decision that imposed a new regime of marriage law on the entire country, Justice Kennedy appealed once again to the premise of *Casey* (as further developed in the 2003 case *Lawrence v. Texas*) in an opinion that treated the human person as a bundle of desires that are coterminous with rights, desires whose satisfaction is the primary function of just government. Justice Antonin Scalia, in his *Obergefell* dissent, rightly and witheringly noted that, in Kennedy's opinion for the majority, "[t]he Supreme Court of the United States has descended from the disciplined legal reasoning of John Marshall and Joseph Story to the mystical aphorisms of the fortune cookie." The problem was, and is, worse than that, however.

For whatever one's opinion of the abortion liberty defined by *Casey* or the marriage law mandated by *Obergefell*, what ought to concern all Americans who care about the moral-cultural roots of our democracy is the drastically diminished concept of the human person—the desperately deficient *anthropology*, in the philosophical sense of the term—that underwrites both *Casey* and *Obergefell*. That deficient anthropology reduces human aspiration to the pleasure principle, human choosing to sheer willfulness, and the human person to the sum total of his desires. There is no notion here of what the Founders understood to be lives formed by "sacred Honor", for in the republic of *Casey* and *Obergefell*, one person's honor is another's bigotry, and one person's dishonorable behavior is another's unjustly frustrated desire. There is no claim here that the American democratic experiment rests on self-evident moral truths, which is to say, truths that can be known by reason; for in the anthropology implicit in *Casey* and *Obergefell*, there is only "your truth" and "my truth", but nothing that can properly be described as *the* truth. (And that, I might add, is why the legal regime imposed by the Supreme Court in *Casey* and *Obergefell* had to be, well, *imposed*—because if there is only your truth and my truth, and our truths collide, only an imposition of power will settle the argument between us, for we have no horizon of moral judgment against which to resolve our differences.)

This desperately deficient anthropology is not exclusively located on one end of the conventional ideological spectrum. Although its prominence in our public life is the greatest—in the sense of furthest-reaching—achievement of the cultural left, the notion of freedom-as-willfulness implied by that anthropology is ubiquitous. It can be found on the libertarian right and in parts of the business community. It has conquered most of what used to be called "mainline" Protestantism, and it has made serious inroads into Catholicism in the United States. Within American Jewry, only small enclaves of the Orthodox and the Modern Orthodox retain a notion of freedom as related to something other than personal willfulness.

In 2026, the United States of America will celebrate the 250th anniversary of the Declaration of Independence. Between now and then, we can begin the process of ensuring that, on its Tercentenary in 2076, the American experiment is in recognizable moral-cultural continuity with its founding. But that is possible only if we recognize that that continuity has been severely attenuated—we live less in a democratic republic formed by the fruitful interaction of biblical religion, classical rationality, medieval political theory, and Enlightenment thought than in a Nietzschean republic, where the triumph of the will has led to the transvaluation of values, now imposed by judicial and regulatory fiat.

That's what *happened* in 2016: America looked in the mirror and found, not George Washington, John Adams, James Madison, or Abraham Lincoln, but Friedrich Nietzsche impersonated by Justice Kennedy.

This brings us to the second question: *Now* what?

Historians debate the precise number of "Great Awakenings" that had such a profound effect on both American national culture and politics. There seems to be broad agreement that a First Great Awakening of the 1730s and 1740s set in motion ideas and aspirations that were crucial in forming the national mind and spirit during the American Revolution, and that a Second Great Awakening in the early nineteenth century shaped the social dynamics that were one root of the Civil War. Whether a Third Great Awakening (which some scholars claim took place in the second half of the nineteenth century) was instrumental in producing the politics of early twentieth-century progressivism is still debated. Some even suggest that the Sixties counterculture amounted to a Fourth Great Awakening, although its object of worship was not the God of the Bible, as was the case in the previous Awakenings, however enumerated.

The current crisis of American political culture is not going to be satisfactorily resolved by constitutional amendments (although it's conceivable that some amendments might help rebalance and reanimate an often-dysfunctional and overbearing national government). Nor is the current crisis going to be satisfactorily resolved by a rollback of the regulatory state, or a return to the gold standard, or a massive public works program, or a devolution of educational choice to parents, although sensible arguments can be made in favor of each of those proposals.

Why? Because politics and law cannot resolve America's anthropological crisis—that is, the American crisis in the idea of the human person. Politics and law can stop exacerbating that crisis. Politics and law can stop impeding efforts to address it. But politics and law cannot resolve the crisis, because politics and law of themselves cannot revitalize the cultural subsoil of American democracy from which grow the habits of mind and heart that turn democratic self-governance from an aspiration to a capacity.

What is needed to resolve the crisis is another Great Awakening.

This new Awakening will be different. While it will depend in considerable part on a renewal of vitality among America's religious communities, it will not be exclusively the project of believers.

Among the believers, Catholics will contribute to it by embracing what the popes of the past quarter-century have called the "New Evangelization", which teaches a radically different view of the human person than today's culture of the imperial autonomous Self. Evangelical Protestants—those who have not mortgaged their public witness to the transient fashions of electoral politics and the allure of proximity to power—will contribute to it by demonstrating, along with their Catholic brethren, that the life of the Beatitudes not only makes for a happier personal and familial life, but for a nobler public life, in which the ideas of solidarity and the common good return to prominence in our public moral culture. American Jewry will contribute to it by disentangling itself from the politics of lifestyle libertinism and reminding us all that the Exodus—the idea of life as pilgrimage and adventure, guided by a moral law that liberates us from the habits of slaves and points us toward a land of humane promise—is *the* foundational image in the Western concept of freedom. Latter-Day Saints will contribute to it by modeling the intentional communities of family, moral conviction, and generous philanthropy in which the new Awakening will be nurtured.

At the same time, the new Awakening will be a retrieval and renewal of those political-philosophical truths that were once alive in the United States, and that proved their contemporary vitality in the 1980s in Central and Eastern Europe, in what we have come to know as the Revolution of 1989. Those truths will be proposed, and worked into the texture of our public life, by nonbelievers as well as religious believers.

Foremost among those truths is the public ideal that Václav Havel called "living in the truth". In Havel's case, and that of the other dissidents who created the revolution of conscience that underlay the political Revolution of 1989, "living in the truth" meant refusing to submit to the Communist culture of the lie by even seemingly unimportant acts of acquiescence, like robotically repeating Communist slogans. For Havel and those who defined the liberating "power of the powerless", living in the truth meant living "as if" one were free. Today, those inspired by Havel and his colleagues, nonbelievers as well as believers, will live "as if" there were truths built into the world and into us, truths that we can know by reason. For "living in the truth", in the new Awakening that can revitalize American public moral culture, will mean recognizing that what is often described as a decline or abandonment of democratic *values* is in fact the decline and abandonment of the *truths* about the human person that are essential to democratic self-governance.

What are the truths that will permit us to "live in the truth"?

Among the most important for the healing of a deeply wounded political culture is the truth that each of us has an inherent dignity and value that is not ascribed by government but that is built into us—a dignity and value that Thomas Jefferson would have called "unalienable".

And the truth that recognizing this built-in dignity and value discloses certain moral obligations and responsibilities, including the obligation to contribute to the common good and the responsibility of living in solidarity with others, especially those who find living their obligations and fulfilling their responsibilities difficult.

And the truth that to think of ourselves and others as twitching bundles of commensurable and morally inconsequential desires is not an act of tolerance, but an exercise in self-abasement that reduces us to an infantilism lethal to democratic self-governance.

And the truth that the good life is not measured solely, or even primarily, in financial terms.

And the truth that a vulgar popular culture appealing to the basest of our instincts is likely to produce a vulgarized political culture in which those base instincts dominate.

The shortest route to the reclamation of those truths is through rediscovering the truth about the human person disclosed in biblical religion, which means turning to the God of the Bible in order to grasp the truth about the human person. But that is not the only path to those truths, as the experience of both the eighteenth and twentieth centuries proves. Thus the coalition of those who can begin the process of a new Great Awakening aimed at the healing of American political culture will be a coalition of believers and unbelievers, people "resolved to speak out clearly and pay up personally", as Albert Camus put it to a group of Dominican monks in 1948—people who are willing to proclaim, and live, a different, nobler view of the human person than the infantile caricature proposed by the culture of the imperial autonomous Self.

Those of us who have been involved for over a quarter-century in the project of creating a religiously informed public philosophy for the American experiment in ordered liberty must admit, in light of 2016, that our project has not succeeded. But what failures there have been have not been due to a fundamentally flawed analysis that failed to get to the root of the matter. On the contrary, the project in which many of us have been engaged has always been based on the understanding that politics is a function of culture, which carries with it the clear implication that a sick public moral culture will yield a sick political culture. That judgment has been vindicated all too well, and the question now is one of remedies at both the political and cultural levels.

But some would even reject that. In recent years, there has been a lot of talk in certain circles about what journalist Rod Dreher has dubbed the "Benedict Option". According to the Benedict Option, political remedies to our national crisis have proven unavailing, and Christians of all denominational persuasions would be foolish to put further time and effort into trying to reconstruct American politics. Rather, they should learn from what Dreher and others take to be the example of Saint Benedict of Nursia, a monk of the so-called Dark Ages, and withdraw from political contestation while building intentional communities of virtue based on the truths that make for genuine human flourishing. The signs of the times, proponents of the Benedict Option tell us, make the task ahead clear: abandon all hope for a political solution to what is a civilizational crisis and turn toward the construction of virtuous life in self-organized small communities. For it is there that the seeds of civilizational rebirth will be planted, much as they were when Benedictine monasteries saved the civilizational memory of the West and gave birth to medieval Christendom.

There are important truths here, and they should be acknowledged. Yes, we are in a profound moral-cultural or civilizational crisis. True, politics will not get us to the root of the crisis, and the political process is unlikely to be an agent of either cultural healing or cultural regeneration. Yes, intentional communities where virtuous men and women can lead noble lives are a worthy aspiration; and, as Yuval Levin has argued powerfully in *The Fractured Republic*, those communities may well become laboratories for a new politics that resists the claims of the Leviathan state and recognizes the importance of the principle of subsidiarity in democratic life. All this can be readily conceded.

Indeed, learning—or perhaps more accurately, rediscovering— these truths about the importance of community and the limits of politics is essential to the task of reviving a moral culture conducive to freedom properly understood. That is as true today as it was two millennia ago, as anyone who ponders Matthew 22:21 and its instruction about who gets rendered what will understand. It was true in Augustine's fifth century, and in Benedict's sixth century. It was true in medieval Christendom. It was true in the nineteenth century, as revolutions swept away the old European order. It was certainly true during the murderous twentieth century. And it was true in the early years of this twenty-first century, as Richard Neuhaus and others reminded believers that the first public task of the Church is to be itself—the Church—and not a partisan sect or the chaplaincy to a political party. Insofar as the Benedict Option embodies these long-held truths, it can be both catalyst and ally in a new Awakening.

Yet proponents of the Benedict Option would do well to rethink several things. To begin with, this so-called Ben-Op, at least as imagined by some, misreads the history of the second half of the first millennium. Yes, the monasteries along the Atlantic littoral helped preserve the civilizational patrimony of the West when public order in Western Europe broke down and the Norsemen wrought havoc along the Atlantic seaboard and beyond. But Monte Cassino, the great motherhouse of Saint Benedict's reforming spiritual movement, was never completely cut off from the life around it, and over the centuries it helped educate thinkers of the civilization-forming caliber of Thomas Aquinas.

Moreover, the Benedictine Rule developed at Monte Cassino inspired men like a young Roman patrician named Gregorius, who, after leaving the world of public affairs for which he had been trained, founded a monastery based on the Rule of Saint Benedict in the Eternal City. But he was eventually called back to ecclesial and public service, and the man whom history would know as Pope Saint Gregory the Great became both Bishop of Rome and de facto civic leader. And as pope, while attending to the affairs of both the city and the Church, he sent another monk, the abbot of the monastery Gregory had founded, to evangelize England; that monk we now know as Saint Augustine of Canterbury. So perhaps we should think of a "Gregorian Option", in which intentional communities become the launchpads for education, cultural and social renewal, and evangelization, rather than a "Benedict Option" misconstrued as a withdrawal from the world, its snares, and its delusions.

The proponents of the Benedict Option rightly criticize the way in which some Christian leaders have failed to speak truth to political power because they have become enthralled with the promise of proximity to that power. There were certainly enough examples to illustrate their point in the 2016 electoral cycle. But men and women of conviction and conscience may still be found in our state legislatures and in Congress, among the state governors, and in the administration of the federal government. They deserve more than the support of believers' prayers, offered from the safety of auto-constructed twenty-first-century catacombs and other enclaves; they deserve the engaged support of citizens who know full well that politics and law cannot fix what is broken in our public moral culture, but who also know that a political and legal framework for national cultural renewal must be created, at least in terms of creating free space for that moral-cultural renewal to unfold.

Christians are still called to be salt and light in the world, and to care actively for the common good (cf. Mt 5:13–16). To approach politics without illusions is an imperative of Christian realism. To abandon political life entirely is to default on one's obligations to solidarity and the common good—and, ultimately, to the virtue of charity.

A kind of parallel to the Benedict Option may be found in those thinkers who have essentially opted out of the contemporary political fray on the grounds that the United States is an ill-founded republic with a deeply flawed political-philosophical DNA. John Locke is typically the evil villain here, and from Locke's epistemology and political theory these scholars draw a straight line to the current national moral-cultural and political crisis, as embodied in the enshrinement of the imperial autonomous Self at the heart of American democracy and the *Casey* and *Obergefell* decisions.

Although I fully share these thinkers' disdain for the debased idea of the human person that underwrites *Casey* and *Obergefell*—because, like them, I think that idea a prescription for both personal unhappiness and societal decay—the line from John Locke's individualism to Anthony Kennedy's autonomous Self seems rather less straight to me.

As Ryan Anderson and others have pointed out, the American founding was much more than John Locke, and the new Awakening being proposed here will recognize that. The American founding involved public aspects of the Puritan heritage, including its communitarianism. The founding drew on the English common-law tradition, the roots of which may be found in medieval Catholic political theory. Classical thought played its role in the founding, especially the Ciceronian conviction that personal and civic virtue and the rule of law are mutually reinforcing. So to suggest, as the ill-founded republic theorists do, that the founding was exclusively a product of the Enlightenment is to indulge in a very truncated notion of the history of Western political thought. Indeed, it can be argued (and has been quite extensively by the Anglo-American historian of ideas Larry Siedentop) that certain ideas essential to the democratic project—the equal dignity and equal capacity for virtue of all human beings, the distinction between spiritual and temporal power, the principle of consent in governance, even the notion of "natural" or built-in rights—find their deepest roots in Christianity. The new Awakening capable of renewing and reforming America's public moral culture, and thus America's political culture, will be fed from the multiple streams that fed the founding, although forming from those sources a new moral-cultural synthesis.

Moreover, there are more than four hundred years of history between Locke and *Obergefell*, and while ideas clearly have consequences for good and ill, politics is shaped by more than ideas. It is shaped by experience. And while I hope it's clear that I do not underrate the importance of ideas in public life, I might also suggest that an experience of affluence that is not tempered by a public moral culture that honors self-discipline and instills an ethic of responsibility for those left behind has rather more to do with the contemporary state of American political culture than Locke's *Essay Concerning Human Understanding* and his *Two Treatises of Government*.

Reforming our moral culture will require a short game and a long game. If, because of the results of the 2016 election, Leviathan is kept at bay for a while, the regulatory state is reined in, and the Supreme Court is reconfigured so that it no longer functions as Leviathan's superlegislature, space will have been created for immediate short-game action that addresses some urgent issues. That short game will include a deepened critique of vulgarity and rapaciousness that does not fall into the trap of dismissing markets as inevitably corrupting. It will include a critique of the inherently demagogic character of social media and their current impact on public life, while working to develop a new public culture of conversation and debate that gets America out of the brackish shallows of demagogy and into the deeper and more bracing waters of serious debate. This short game will also include a recognition that our politics—in the narrowest, electoral sense of the term—has too often devolved into the selection of authorized poachers who are expected to bring home as much game as possible from the public game preserve. But in recognizing and critiquing that, the short game will also challenge those who now suggest that efficient authoritarianism is the answer to our public woes.

The long game is, of course, the more important and determinative game. The long game is the new Great Awakening: the rebirth of the ideas about the human person, human community, and human destiny that once informed the American experiment in ordered liberty, that can inform it again—and that must do so, if the American republic of 2076 is to stand in vital moral and cultural continuity with the American republic of 1776.

That new Awakening, to repeat, will be the project of believers and unbelievers, and it will involve men and women of good will across a good portion of the conventional political spectrum. The new Awakening will be resisted by those for whom the sole meaning and purpose of American democracy is the satisfaction of the desires of the autonomous Self; it will also be resisted by those for whom democracy is a failed experiment to be remedied by a new authoritarianism. But neither of those centers of resistance has a viable proposal for the American future. For the Selfers are committed to an imposition of their deconstructive project that inevitably leads to a kind of dictatorship of relativism, while those flirting with a new authoritarianism will discover the lesson that the mid-twentieth century ought to have taught them: the messiness of democracy is preferable to the jackboot and the cudgel.

The task is to see that this democratic messiness does not completely devolve into democratic dysfunction. And that requires the rebuilding of a true culture of freedom.

In his inaugural address, President John F. Kennedy noted that "in the long history of the world, only a few generations have been granted the role of defending freedom in its hour of maximum danger." That challenge was met, and freedom was vindicated, in the Revolution of 1989 and the collapse of European Communism. Now freedom must be defended against another grave danger: the danger posed by a profound misunderstanding of freedom, which threatens to become freedom's undoing.

The weapons in this new struggle will be, in the main, the weapons of the spirit and the intellect. But then, in the final analysis, those were the weapons that forged the distinctive victory of the West in the Cold War. The new Awakening that can meet the challenge of securing the future of freedom in the face of the many solvents that now threaten it will be a multigenerational task. It will certainly not be completed in our lifetimes, and probably not in our children's. But the next Great Awakening is crucial to the flourishing, even the survival, of the American experiment in ordered liberty, so it must be begun. And so, to revert once again to Kennedy in January 1961, "Let us begin."

# Part Three

# The Church in the Postmodern World

# The Signs of These Times

## *John Paul II and the Renovation of Christian Humanism*

The canonization of Pope John Paul II on April 27, 2014, nine years after his holy death, was the occasion to remember a spiritually radiant personality: a Catholic priest and bishop who, contrary to all expectations, captured the world's imagination and held it for more than a quarter-century. Indeed, the canonization ceremony might be considered a moment at which the Church's official leadership caught up with the spontaneous judgment of the Church's people, which was rendered by chants of "Santo subito!" (Sainthood now!) at John Paul's funeral Mass on April 8, 2005. That John Paul's Christian witness had touched innumerable lives was also made clear by the numbers of pilgrims who came to Rome for the canonization, as well as by the many letters, some simply addressed "Pope John Paul II/Heaven", that found their way to the Office of the Cause of the Beatification and Canonization of the Servant of God John Paul II in the Vicariate of Rome—some of which came from non-Christians and nonbelievers. The fact that John Paul II's life of heroic virtue affected men and women across the religious and political spectrums contributed to making his canonization, like that of Saint Teresa of Calcutta, a moment of genuine ecumenical and interreligious encounter.

And yet, amid the celebration, there were the usual dissenters who continued to insist that this was a pope who had dragged the Church backwards, intellectually and pastorally, in a pontificate of "restoration" that betrayed the Second Vatican Council's promise of a new Catholic dialogue with modernity. As they had done since the early 1980s, these countervoices insisted that Karol Wojtyła had a premodern cast of mind, and that his pontificate thus ill-suited the modern (or postmodern) world—a mantra picked up by the less-alert sectors of the global media. Yet anyone who has taken the trouble to look seriously into both Wojtyła's pre-papal life as well as his pontificate would have to conclude that this indictment is mistaken.

"Premodern" simply is not an adequate category through which to understand the intellectual development of a man who, in the late 1940s, was dissatisfied with aspects of the neo-Scholastic theology in which he had been trained. "Premodern" cannot adequately describe a scholar who deliberately chose to study the phenomenology of Max Scheler for his second doctoral thesis, or who was a vigorous participant in efforts to renew philosophical anthropology throughout the 1950s. Nor does it seem appropriate to call "premodern" one of the most intellectually engaged bishops in Europe in the years before and after Vatican II. Karol Wojtyła was a man who deliberately sought the intellectual companionship of philosophers, theologians, historians, scientists, and artists from a wide range of intellectual perspectives; a man who, as both pastor and scholar, displayed a deep sympathy for those caught in the modern crisis of belief; a man who avidly read contemporary philosophy and literature for more than a half-century.

Then there is the record of his pontificate. Would a pope with a "premodern" intellectual perspective have written the first papal encyclical on Christian anthropology, making the renovation of Christian humanism the leitmotif and program of his pontificate? It seems unlikely. Would a "premodern" pope have defended the universality of human rights before the United Nations in 1979 and 1995, while transforming the Catholic Church into perhaps the world's foremost institutional promoter of the democratic project? It seems unlikely. Would a "premodern" pope have underscored the importance of free and uncoerced assent to religious belief in an encyclical on the imperative of Christian mission, writing that "the Church proposes; she imposes nothing"? Would a pope who lived, intellectually, in the premodern world have given the Church an empirically sensitive social magisterium in which there is no hint of nostalgia for the world of the ancien régime? Would a "premodern" pope have written an international best seller in which he openly described philosophy's "turn to the subject" as irreversible, or an encyclical that acutely analyzed the condition in which human reason finds itself three centuries after that epic "turn"? It all seems very unlikely.

Nor does it seem likely that a "premodern" pope would have visited the Great Synagogue of Rome and the Umayyad Grand Mosque in Damascus, called world religious leaders together twice for days of prayer in Assisi, and (against considerable internal opposition) achieved full diplomatic relations between the Holy See and the State of Israel. A "premodern" pope would not have insisted that the Catholic Church honestly confront the Galileo case and its subsequent effects on the dialogue between the Church and science. A "premodern" pope would not have hosted seminars that included agnostic and atheistic philosophers, historians, and scientists at the papal summer residence of Castel Gandolfo. A "premodern" pope would most certainly not have described sexual love within the bond of marital fidelity as an icon of the interior life of God the Holy Trinity. And no "premodern" pope would ever have told the leadership of the Roman Curia that the Church of discipleship formed in the image of a woman, Mary, has a certain theological priority over the Church of authority and jurisdiction formed in the image of a man, Peter.

The facts simply do not support the notion that Karol Wojtyła was a "premodern" pope whose mentality and teaching grated unbearably on modern consciousness. This mistaken critique of John Paul II also misses the originality of his challenge to late modernity and postmodernity. John Paul did not propose a return to the "premodern" world. Rather, he proposed a thoroughly modern *alternative* reading of modernity. John Paul II's thought and his teaching were a challenge to look at the modern world, its triumphs and its struggles, through a different, and perhaps sharper, lens.

That challenge was crystallized in *Fidei Depositum*, the 1992 apostolic constitution with which John Paul II issued the *Catechism of the Catholic Church*. In that very personal document, John Paul spoke of the symphonic nature of truth, which was an essential aspect of the late Pope's thought and action. For as a man who was first and foremost a disciple of Jesus Christ, and as a scholar who analyzed the teachings of the Catholic Church with contemporary intellectual methods, Karol Wojtyła was convinced that Christian faith has a unity. The Creed is not a random inventory of truth claims—neither is it a "system" constructed by human ingenuity. Rather, Catholic faith for John Paul II was, is, and always will be a unified understanding of the human condition that begins in God's revelation, which is the source of doctrine and the starting point of theology. Here, the Pope reflected an ancient Catholic sensibility. In the symphony of truth that constitutes the faith once delivered to the saints, the "instruments" that make up the ensemble do not perform in a haphazard or incoherent way but support each other in a melodic structure that, by its very nature, demands to be engaged as a whole.

And here lay a series of challenges to key elements of the intellectual sensibility of postmodernism.

The postmodern sensibility typically begins and ends its reading of ancient texts with the historical-critical method, leading many postmoderns to claim that it is impossible for Christians today to have access to the origins of the Church. John Paul II's magisterium, which affirmed historical-critical scholarship as an important tool of biblical interpretation, nonetheless suggested an alternative reading of our situation: the Church is never cut off from the sources of faith, because the living Christ is always present to the Church.

Then there are those postmodern radical pluralists for whom discontinuity is the hallmark of human history. From his personal experience as well as through his study of history, John Paul II recognized that the human project frequently takes unexpected turns, even in the course of a single lifetime. Yet the Pope nevertheless taught an alternative reading of our circumstances. Although Christian faith is symphonic, an ensemble of truths rather than a solo instrument, it nonetheless maintains its unity over time and space. Despite differences of language, culture, and historical moment, the authentic Christian truth preached in the twenty-first century is the truth once given to the apostles. That, too, is a datum of revelation, for it reflects Christ's promise that the Holy Spirit will preserve the Church in Christ's truth. Moreover, it is a datum of revelation that can be confirmed by those forms of contemporary historical scholarship that do not begin with an unwarranted assumption of the radical discontinuity of human experience.

Elements of moral truth form part of the symphony of truth that is Catholic faith in its fullness, and they offer yet another important challenge to postmodern moral relativism. From his first steps as a professorial lecturer in moral philosophy until the last years of his pontificate, Karol Wojtyła, whose approach to the moral life was shaped by both extensive pastoral experience and intense reflection, challenged the radical relativists who may grudgingly concede that in matters of the moral life there may be "your" truth and "my" truth, but who also insist that there is certainly no such thing as "the truth" *stricte dictu*. John Paul II had an alternative view of our moral situation. He was convinced that a careful philosophical reflection on human moral agency revealed truths that are built into the world and into human beings: truths that feed the human mind and soul, truths we ignore at grave peril to ourselves and to the human project.

In all of this, John Paul II challenged postmodern theories that presupposed the futility of our search for truth with a coherent understanding of the Christian proposal, in which the various affirmations of the Creed are clarified in their relationship to each other and to the whole. The men and women of the twenty-first century were not, he believed, condemned to live in a world that is fragmented, cut off from the past, and ultimately incomprehensible. There was an alternative reading of modernity. And that, John Paul II was convinced, was what the Second Vatican Council intended the Catholic Church to propose: a rereading of the contemporary situation in which the modern world's intense reflection on the human person would be revitalized through an encounter with Christ, who reveals both the face of the merciful Father *and* the true meaning of our humanity.

The bloody twentieth century demonstrated beyond doubt that the great humanistic project of the past several centuries had been derailed. The Church's great service to the late modern world, Karol Wojtyła believed, was to help rescue the humanistic project through a Christ-centered humanism. That is what Bishop Wojtyła wrote to the Vatican commission preparing the agenda of Vatican II. That was Wojtyła's understanding of the Council as he experienced it from 1962 to 1965. That was the program he advanced in his implementation of the Council in Kraków. And that was the understanding of Vatican II that guided his pontificate. John Paul II was not interested in the restoration of a premodern Church, in any sense of the term "restoration". He was passionately committed to the proclamation of a thoroughly modern Christian humanism that allows the Church to address the civilizational crisis of our times.

John Paul II's alternative construction of modernity was also evident in his distinctively Slavic reading of history, which ran parallel to that of another great Slavic witness to the dignity of man, Aleksandr Solzhenitsyn. In his 1983 Templeton Prize Lecture, previously noted in these pages, Solzhenitsyn tried to locate the root of the evils of the twentieth century. Why did a century that had begun with robust confidence in the human future so quickly decay into the greatest epoch of slaughter in human history? What accounted for the fact that a century bright with expectation had by its midpoint produced two world wars, three totalitarian systems, a Cold War that threatened catastrophe on a planetary scale, oceans of blood, and mountains of corpses? There were obviously a host of factors at work, but beneath them all Solzhenitsyn discerned a profound truth: "Men have forgotten God." In a twenty-first-century world in which distorted religious convictions are themselves twisted into warrants for savagery and terrorism, it can seem a diagnosis that hints at a cure worse than the disease. But that is to mistake Solzhenitsyn's distinctive Slavic reading of history, which John Paul II shared, for a simplistic (or, once again, a supposedly "premodern") religiosity. It's a mistake that misses something terribly important.

In a Slavic view of the world, culture—not politics, and not economics—is the dynamic engine of history over time. And at the heart of "culture" is "cult": what we cherish, what we esteem, what we worship. If the object of our worship is false—and the pretense that a thoroughly modern mind has no need of worship is itself the worship of a false god, the self-constituting Self—culture will inevitably become corrupt. And when a corrupt culture, including desperately defective ideas about the human person, is married to modern technology, the result is human suffering on an unprecedented scale. That, at bottom, is why the twentieth century unfolded the way it did. The barbarism stemmed from the fact that men, having forgotten God, forgot who and what they were, and could be.

John Paul II agreed with those who have been arguing for some years now that secularization is not a neutral phenomenon. A thoroughly secularized world is a world without windows, doors, or skylights—claustrophobic, and ultimately suffocating. A thoroughly secularized culture from which transcendent reference points for human thought and action have disappeared is bad for the cause of human freedom and democracy, because democracy finally rests on two convictions: that the human person possesses an inalienable dignity and value, and that freedom is not mere willfulness. At an even more profound level, a thoroughly secularized world is bad for human beings. "Silence," as the very progressive German cardinal Karl Lehmann once put it to me, "is stifling: Human beings cannot live with the silence."

This brings us back to John Paul II's alternative reading of the modern condition and his Christian humanism. In John Paul's vision of the human person and of history, the question of God remains central precisely because the question of man is and always will be central. To ask the question of man is, inevitably, to raise the question of God. To try to read the course of history without God is to read history in a shallow way, because God's search for man and the human response to that divine quest is the central reality of history. To ask, "What is man, and how does the human person function in history?" is to confront the question of God. A true anthropology, a true humanism, speaks of "God-and-man", and thus liberates men and women from the stifling confines of "the silence".

Immersing myself in the life and thought of Karol Wojtyła during the preparation of *Witness to Hope* and its sequel, *The End and the Beginning,* and in many hours of personal conversation with John Paul II over more than a decade, I became convinced that what Cardinal Joseph Ratzinger once called John Paul's "passion for man" was formed in the cauldron of the Second World War. There and then, he decided to spend out his life in defense of the dignity and value of every human life, and to do so through the priesthood of the Catholic Church. There and then, he committed himself to helping build what he later called a "culture of life" to stand against the late modern world's many manifestations of what he perceived as a "culture of death"—and he committed himself to doing so, not against modernity, but by means of a more authentic, thoroughly modern humanism. He could not have known, in 1945, where that commitment would lead him. But that the commitment remained constant while his life's journey unfolded along a sometimes surprising course cannot be denied by anyone who studies that remarkable life carefully.

These convictions about Christ-centered humanism are also the key to understanding John Paul II's influence on the history of the late twentieth century and the early twenty-first. During the latter years of the pontificate, when John Paul became an international celebrity of a distinctive sort, one often got the impression that some commentators wanted to "split" the Pope, setting the "good" Pope-as-defender-of-human-rights over against the "disturbing" Pope-who-defended-the-teaching-of-the-Catholic-Church. But this was to misread completely what friends and critics alike recognized as a remarkably integrated personality. Moreover, that misreading of Wojtyła leads to a misreading of his times, and ours.

It was precisely because of his convictions about God, Christ, culture, and history that the Pope could ignite the revolution of conscience in Central and Eastern Europe that we now know as the Revolution of 1989. It was precisely because John Paul II was convinced that God is central to the story of man that he could, by calling men and women to religious and moral conversion, give them tools of resistance that Communism could not blunt. It was precisely because John Paul II understood that Christianity is not a form of religious idealism, existing somewhere outside history, that he could call people to solidarity in history—and thereby change the course of history. Stalin's famously derisive challenge to the papacy—"The pope? How many divisions does he have?"—was met by a man who knew and understood the power of truth in history, which is another way of describing the power of God in history. And because of that, as Mikhail Gorbachev admitted, Stalin's empire was dismantled nonviolently.

Faith in God can and does transform the world. Faith in the God-made-visible in the world through the person and work of Jesus Christ is liberating. Confidence in the capacities of the men and women whose possibilities for goodness have been revealed in Christ can change the course of history for the better. There is truth beyond "the silence", and it is liberating truth.

There is one other crucial aspect of John Paul II's alternative reading of modernity. So much of modern and postmodern thought teaches us that the royal road to human happiness lies in self-assertion. Karol Wojtyła had a different understanding of the road to human flourishing: he believed it lay along the path of self-giving. That none of us is the cause of our own existence was, for John Paul II, far more than an elementary fact of biology. It is a biological fact that, reflected upon critically and carefully, reveals a deep truth about the human person: We find the truth about ourselves in making ourselves into the gift-for-others that our own lives are to us. The self-giving self, not the self-asserting self, is the truly human self.

Wojtyła believed that this deep truth of the human condition could be demonstrated philosophically; at the same time, he understood it to be a central conviction of Christian faith. That is why, for him, the martyr was the highest form of Christian witness, for in martyrdom the complete gift-of-self coincides in the most radical possible way with the convictions to which one has given one's life. In a world Church whose most precious heritage from the twentieth century includes the millions of names in the modern book of martyrs, this conviction of John Paul II about the centrality of self-gift to a true understanding of the human condition ought to strike a powerful chord.

Whatever the fragmentation that besets every human life, every man and woman yearns to live with an undivided heart. Karol Wojtyła, Pope John Paul II, was a thoroughly modern man with a great reverence for the past. As archival materials from Communist-era secret police files made unmistakably clear, he was a man who knew human wickedness and the enduring power of evil in history. Yet he was able to overcome evil with the power of truth and with a shrewd sense of how the "children of light" ought to work in and through history to bend the course of events in a more humane direction. He was neither a naïf nor a romantic; he knew that suffering and death are the universal human lot; and yet he showed in his own dying that suffering conformed to Christ can be ennobling and inspiring.

Above all, John Paul II was a Christian disciple who lived out the conviction that Jesus Christ is the answer to the question that is every human life. That conviction shaped an undivided and very large heart, a life of heroic virtue, and a striking analysis of our postmodern cultural circumstance. And while a life of heroic virtue is what the Catholic Church officially acknowledged in canonizing Karol Wojtyła, his distinctive reading of the signs of these times is an essential part of the challenge that Saint John Paul II posed, and continues to pose, to twenty-first-century culture and twenty-first-century public life.

# Synod-2014

## The Church's German Problem, Africa's Catholic Moment, and the Global Crisis of Marriage and the Family

On November 19, 1964, the draft text of Vatican II's Declaration on Religious Freedom was abruptly pulled from the floor of the Council and a vote on it deferred for a year. The announcement of this unexpected decision, prompted by a request from Italian and Spanish bishops thought to be opposed to the declaration, led to something approaching chaos. A petition to Pope Paul VI was hastily cobbled together and signed by hundreds of Council Fathers, asking the Pope to permit a vote on the declaration before the Council adjourned its third period in two days' time. Paul VI determined that, despite the complaints of the majority, conciliar procedure had not been violated and the vote would be deferred until the Council's fourth period in the fall of 1965, at which point, Paul VI promised, the declaration would be the first item on the agenda.

Nothing like this legendary Black Thursday (which that patrician Latinist, John Courtney Murray, preferred to call the *dies irae*, the "day of wrath") had been seen in the Catholic Church in the intervening fifty years until another Thursday: October 16, 2014, near the conclusion of the Extraordinary Synod on the Family convoked by Pope Francis to prepare an agenda for the Ordinary Synod on the Family scheduled to meet in October 2015. (In Vatican-speak, Synod-2015 was deemed "ordinary" because it was one of the regularly scheduled Synods that take place every three or four years.) The Synod meeting of October 2014, which involved presidents of national bishops' conferences around the world and other senior Catholic officials, was indeed extraordinary, not least because, on October 16, the Fathers of Synod-2014 staged a mass revolt in the

Synod Hall. There, amid another dramatic scene that included raised and angry voices, the Fathers forced the Synod leadership to release the full texts of the reports of their language-based discussion groups, many of which had been highly critical of the Interim Report issued after the Synod's first week of plenary debate. That majority revolt, in turn, set in motion a process that led to a much modified, and considerably improved, Final Report from Synod-2014.

In both these instances, the outbreak of very un-Roman behavior indicated that something serious was afoot, something that involved the very self-understanding of the Catholic Church. In 1964, the topic was religious freedom, but the deeper issues were the nature of the human person, the relationship between the rights of conscience and the claims of truth, the historic relationship of the Church to state power, and Catholicism's evolving attitude toward political modernity. In 2014, the topic was the family and the Church's pastoral response to the sexual revolution, but the underlying disputed questions were almost exactly the same, although this time they involved the Church's relationship to postmodern culture more than its relationship to democracy and the separation of church and state.

Alas, very little of that depth was apparent in the reporting and commentary on Synod-2014, which was too frequently filtered through the narrative prism of "humane, progressive pope and his allies *vs.* throwbacks to the party of intransigence at Vatican II". That storyline, however, involved a misconception of the real issues engaged, a false portrait of the Synod majority, a pattern of denial about the manipulations that marred the Synod process, and a cartoonish caricature of those cast in the role of Bad Guys. Worst of all, it diverted attention from the grave matters Pope Francis quite correctly wished to bring to the fore: the crisis of marriage and the family throughout the West, and the challenge of linking truth and mercy in the pastoral care of those damaged in countless ways by this crisis.

Pope Francis' call for two Synods on the family certainly reflected a keen understanding that there is a global crisis of marriage, as he made clear in a passionate address to the Schoenstatt movement the week after Synod-2014 concluded. There, he observed that marriage and family have never been so attacked as they are today, by a "throwaway culture" that reduces the covenant of marriage to a mere "association", and against which the Church must propose "very clearly" the truth about marriage. It seemed to have been the Pope's intention that the 2014 Extraordinary Synod be a wide-ranging discussion of the crisis of marriage and the family—for only if the nature of the crisis is understood in full can the Church proceed to think about how it can propose its understanding of marriage in ways that can be more readily heard and lived in today's Gnostic culture. But if a thorough examination of the crisis, and the celebration of Christian marriage as the answer to it, was indeed Francis' intention for Synod-2014, that intention was largely frustrated, thanks in no small part to German bishops led by retired Cardinal Walter Kasper, in league with the Synod general secretary, Cardinal Lorenzo Baldisseri, who seemed determined to push the question of Holy Communion for divorced and civilly remarried Catholics to the front of the Synod's debates.

The German fixation on this issue was in one sense an expression of the self-absorption of the sclerotic German Church with its own pastoral problems, which are indisputably grave. In another sense, however, the "Communion ban" issue (as it was vulgarly described in the press) was a stalking horse for a much larger argument about the nature of doctrine and its development. And this, in turn, meant a reprise of the long-running debate over the meaning of Vatican II and its relationship to Catholic tradition that Kasper and his allies had long fostered and seemed determined to reopen through the mechanism of the Synod.

Ten months before Synod-2014 met, I asked a knowledgeable observer of German Catholic affairs why the German Catholic leadership insisted on revisiting the issue of Holy Communion for those in civil second marriages. Most of the rest of the world Church thought that question had been sufficiently aired in the 1980 Synod on the Family, and the issue seemed to have been settled by the reaffirmation of the Church's traditional teaching and practice in Saint John Paul II's 1981 apostolic exhortation, *Familiaris Consortio*, and in the 1983 Code of Canon Law. My question about the German fixation on all this got a one-word answer: "Money."

The German Church is funded by the *Kirchensteuer*, the "church tax" collected by the Federal Republic from every citizen who has not taken action to opt out of it. The funds involved are considerable; in 2011, for example, the *Kirchensteuer* provided the Catholic Church in Germany with $6.3 billion. Recently, however, more and more German Catholics have been choosing to opt out. In a clumsy attempt to stanch the bleeding, the German bishops issued a decree in 2012, stating that anyone who opts out of the tax has "left the Church" and that such de facto apostates are cut off from the Church's sacramental life, except in danger of death. The decree was widely mocked and German canonists declared it a nonstarter, for it takes more to "leave the Church" than signing a civil affidavit. In any event, payment of the *Kirchensteuer* has continued to drop.

Many German bishops seem to have concluded that this pattern of defection from payment of the church tax can best be explained by the perception of the Catholic Church as a mean, narrow, and cruel exponent of propositions that no self-respecting twenty-first-century European can accept, propositions like the indissolubility of marriage. That people have stopped paying the *Kirchensteuer* because they have stopped believing that Jesus is Lord and that the Catholic Church is his Body might seem the more straightforward explanation. But adopting that interpretation would require acknowledging that the meltdown of Catholic faith and practice in Germany has had something to do with the colossal failures of German theology and catechetics to transmit the Gospel effectively under the challenging conditions of late modernity and postmodernity. And that, to borrow an image from another battle involving Germans, seems a bridge too far.

Prior to Synod-2014, extensive critiques of Cardinal Kasper's proposals for allowing divorced Catholics in civil second marriages to be restored to the Church's full eucharistic Communion were published in the theological quarterly *Nova et Vetera* and in a book of essays, *Remaining in the Truth of Christ: Marriage and Communion in the Catholic Church*, whose authors included five scholar-cardinals. In both cases, the responses to the Kasper proposals were academically serious and respectful in tone. Yet Kasper, in replying to his critics (primarily in press interviews), failed to sustain the debate at the level of seriousness it deserved, dismissing those who found grave biblical, patristic, theological, canonical, and pastoral problems with his proposals as doctrinal and scriptural fundamentalists.

During the Synod itself, Cardinal Kasper decamped to Vienna and gave a lecture in which he located his position on marriage and the family within his understanding of Vatican II as a council that had opened a new era in Catholic life, one in which all the old verities are now subject to reexamination, and perhaps even reconsideration. But here, too, one wondered just what information was reaching Germany in recent decades. The vibrant parts of Catholicism in the developed world are those that have lived the dynamic orthodoxy displayed in the teaching of John Paul II and Benedict XVI; the crumbling parts of European Catholicism—which is to say, most of Western European Catholicism, and especially German-speaking Catholicism—are those that have bent to the winds of the postmodern *Zeitgeist* and have fudged the Church's doctrinal and moral boundaries, imagining that to be the "spirit of Vatican II". Yet there was Kasper, in league with Synod general secretary Baldisseri, promoting a further fudging of the boundaries, and doing so in ways that seemed to the majority of Synod Fathers (the media spin notwithstanding) to be in flat contradiction to the teaching of the Lord himself.

In 2001, Cardinal Joachim Meisner, then the archbishop of Cologne, told me that the greatest resource German Catholicism had for rebuilding itself in the twenty-first century was the witness of its twentieth-century martyrs. However, the spiritual power of principled resistance is something that many German theologians, bishops, and theologian-bishops (and their fellow travelers) seem not to have pondered very deeply. Acquiescence, followed by surrender, followed by collaboration—that was the disturbing sequence followed by too much of European Catholicism during the Church's contest with the mid-twentieth-century totalitarianisms in Germany and Italy and with their allies in France. The martyrs chose a different way. The path suggested by their countercultural witness surely deserves consideration as Catholicism tries to implement Pope Francis' vision of a "Church permanently in mission" in the face of aggressive secularism and its erosion of marriage and the family.

Not surprisingly, the proposals pressed by the Germans and their allies at Synod-2014 were presented in much of the mainstream media as something bold, fresh, and innovative, when in fact they were stale and shopworn, remnants of a "progressive" Catholicism that had, by any evangelical criterion, manifestly failed in Europe and elsewhere. What *was* new at the Extraordinary Synod—and what helped make it "extraordinary" in the ordinary sense of that word—was the emergence of African Catholicism as a major factor in shaping the future of global Catholicism. Synod Fathers from sub-Saharan Africa were among the leaders in challenging the Kasper proposals, arguing forcefully that the Christian idea of marriage had come to their cultures as a liberating force, especially for women. They also suggested, implicitly if not explicitly, that bishops representing dying local churches ought not be exporting Western decadence to the Global South, where Catholicism was growing exponentially by preaching the truths of the Gospel with compassion but also without compromise.

This took courage, and not only because it exposed the Africans to charges of being culturally backward (or, as Cardinal Kasper rather inelegantly put it, of being in thrall to "taboos"). It also took courage because a lot of the Church in Africa is paid for by German Catholic development agencies, which are extraordinarily well-off and quite generous, thanks to the *Kirchensteuer*. Yet it seemed to men like Cardinal Wilfrid Fox Napier, the Franciscan archbishop of Durban long thought to be aligned with the Catholic left on political and economic issues, that something of exceptional importance was at stake in the Synod's discussion of both marriage and the pastoral care of those who experience same-sex attraction. Thus Napier and others thought it time to blow the whistle, which Napier did with a remarkable denunciation of the Synod's Interim Report and its leak to the press—a courageous call that effectively gave permission for others to say what they really thought about the manipulations of the Synod's discussion that were openly displayed in that report.

Throughout early October 2014, concerns that the Synod process was being manipulated by the general secretary, Cardinal Baldisseri, in league with Archbishop Bruno Forte, the Italian theologian who was the Synod's special secretary, were routinely dismissed as conservative conspiracy-mongering, even by typically sensible Vaticanisti. That was not the tale told by numerous Synod Fathers, however, and it was clearly their frustrations with the process that led to the blowup of October 16 and the subsequent release of the reports of the debates in the Synod's language-based discussion groups, which revealed sharp and extensive disagreement with the line taken in the Interim Report prepared by Archbishop Forte.

The process was defective in numerous ways. The Pope had called, appropriately, for an open and freewheeling debate, which was not altogether characteristic of Catholicism's experience of Synods since the institution was established during Vatican II. But the Synod secretariat declined to release the texts of the Synod Fathers' interventions (speeches) during the first week when the Fathers, auditors, and observers spoke to the entire assembly. Summaries of the debates released by the Vatican Information Service (presumably under the direction of the Synod secretariat) and more than a few of the Synod's daily press conferences were criticized for being exercises in spin rather than accurate renderings of the breadth of the discussion. Those who suggested that more honest reporting was in order were slapped down, and more than a few Synod Fathers came to the conclusion that, as one put it, manipulation of the proceedings was both "manifest and inept", in the sense of being both obvious and, so to speak, stupidly obvious.

But it was Forte's Interim Report that really put iron into the spines of many Synod Fathers. That report was supposed to be a snapshot of the principal themes of the first week's debates in the general Synod assembly, which were to be further explored and refined in the language-based discussion groups during the Synod's second week. But Forte crafted it as a draft of the final Synod document, highlighting issues that would be of greatest interest to an international media eagerly awaiting the Great Catholic Cave-In to the sexual revolution—and found himself, and the Interim Report, essentially disowned by Cardinal Péter Erdő, the Synod's relator (or official summarizer), at the press conference at which the Interim Report was presented.

As one language-based discussion group began its deliberations, one member asked the others, with respect to the Forte-crafted Interim Report's language on pastoral approaches to persons with same-sex attraction, "Did you hear any of this last week?" He got a unanimously negative reply. The Interim Report's adoption of the language of the LGBT insurgency also came in for serious criticism, with Synod Fathers insisting that the Catholic Church does not describe human beings by their desires, whatever they are, and that doing so contradicts the rich Catholic anthropology of the human person, most recently articulated by John Paul II in his inaugural encyclical, *Redemptor Hominis*, and in his *Theology of the Body*.

Which in turn raised another question about the Synod process: Why were no faculty members of the Pontifical John Paul II Institute on Marriage and the Family invited as auditors or observers of Synod-2014? The institute's home base is the Pope's own Roman university, the Lateran; it has faculties around the world; Stanisław Grygiel, the Institute's founding director, and his wife, Ludmilla, had given magnificent papers on the Christian idea of marriage at a European conference on family matters shortly before the Synod. But the Grygiels were not invited to the Synod, nor was the distinguished moral theologian who was the Rome institute's director, Monsignor Livio Melina. Given the ways of the Vatican, these could not have been accidental omissions. It seemed far more likely that these exclusions were deliberately engineered by the Synod's general secretary, Cardinal Baldisseri, presumably uninterested in having the Kasper approach and the Kasper proposals challenged by the magisterium of John Paul II, even though that magisterium had shown itself over the past two decades to have been the Church's most successful response to the sexual revolution and the severe collateral damage that upheaval had done to marriage and the family.

And here, again, the Synod's German Problem, which is also the Church's German Problem, reared its head. During Synod-2014, Cardinal Kasper and allies like Archbishop Forte seemed largely unacquainted with the achievements of the John Paul II Institutes around the world. Those achievements include the development of an intellectually sophisticated and pastorally compelling Catholic anthropology that meets the assault of the sexual revolution, not by acquiescing to it, but by challenging it to a debate over who takes human sexuality more seriously: those who see in faithful and fruitful married love an icon of the interior life of the Trinity, or those who reduce sex to another contact sport.

This intellectual obtuseness was one significant factor in causing what South Africa's Cardinal Napier described as the "irreparable" damage done by Archbishop Forte's Interim Report. Attempts by Cardinal Baldisseri and others to explain the report away as a mere report card on discussion themes were belied by two facts. First, the Interim Report was severely criticized in at least seven of the ten language-based discussion groups in the Synod's second week, where it was regarded as an inaccurate rendering of the Synod's discussions.

Second, very little of what the Catholic left and the world press found revolutionary and agreeable in the Interim Report was to be found in the Synod's Final Report, which Pope Francis declared the agenda-setting document for Synod-2015, or in the Synod's "Message" to the world, a well-crafted document celebrating marriage and the family.

Yet because the Interim Report was leaked before it was formally presented (not accidentally, one presumes), the media template on Synod-2014 was quickly set in concrete ("It's finally happened! The Catholic Church is changing!"). This story line would, in turn, distort and misshape the continuing reflection on marriage and the family that was to have taken place between Synod-2014 and Synod-2015. The damage done by Forte's Interim Report may not have been completely "irreparable", pace Cardinal Napier, but it was certainly severe. And that it did not cost Archbishop Forte his job at Synod-2015 was, in retrospect, telling.

In his closing address to Synod-2014, Pope Francis declared the meeting a success—which it was, if not precisely in the way the Synod minority (the supporters of the Kasper proposals and the Forte Interim Report) subsequently claimed. A robust debate was held in the Synod Hall and on the edges of the Synod despite the difficult circumstances created by the Synod general secretariat. Out of that debate emerged a clear consensus in favor of the Catholic Church's classic teaching on the nature of the human person, the morality of love, the nature of marriage, and the need to combine truth and mercy in proclaiming what John Paul II called the Gospel of Life. Pastors who had been clumsy or cruel in dealing with couples in irregular marriages or with those experiencing same-sex attraction—a distinct minority, in my experience—were reminded that the Good Shepherd remains the model of pastoral charity in the Church. Africa has been a vital center of Catholic life and Catholic witness for decades, and thanks to Synod-2014, that vitality and witness was fully in play at the highest levels of the Church's deliberations. The Pope's call for openness, and the confidence the African bishops displayed in the truth of their own ecclesial experience, empowered them to resist suggestions, not least by Cardinal Kasper, that they defer to their European betters.

And while a lot of the reporting and commentary on Synod-2014 fell back into the tiresome habit of portraying all Catholic debates in the hoary categories of Good Progressives and Bad Conservatives, a closer examination of the debates made it clear to those with eyes to see and ears to hear that the drama of the Catholic Church in the twenty-first century is not unfolding according to the playbook detailed in the now half-century-old *New Yorker* articles by the pseudonymous "Xavier Rynne", who crafted the cowboys-and-Indians clichés that still guide too much mainstream media coverage of matters Catholic. The dynamic and orthodox leaders of the Church today—the men who successfully foiled the attempt to divert Synod-2014 down the path charted by the Interim Report, and whose interventions accounted for the much improved Final Report and the Synod's "Message" to the world—were all men *of* Vatican II, not men *against* Vatican II. They read the Council through the magisterium of John Paul II and Benedict XVI, which they see as offering an authoritative interpretation of its teaching, and they clearly wanted that authoritative interpretation deployed in service to what John Paul II called the New Evangelization—which Pope Francis, in the 2013 apostolic exhortation, *Evangelii Gaudium*, declared the grand strategy of his own pontificate. They know that the New Evangelization is not advanced by tactical, and still less by strategic, compromises with the *Zeitgeist* on the indissolubility of marriage and the morality of human love. And they are not prepared to take instructions on how to advance the New Evangelization from Catholic leaders in Germany, Italy, England, or elsewhere who have manifestly failed in their own evangelical mission.

Still, there were a lot of things that could have been usefully discussed at Synod-2014 and weren't because of the drama described above.

The Synod's work would have been more fruitful if it had been more data-driven than anecdotal. Evidence is abundantly available to demonstrate that the Church's idea of permanent and fruitful marriage, like the Church's teaching on the appropriate means of regulating fertility, makes for happier marriages, happier families, happier children, and more-benevolent societies than does the deconstruction of marriage and the family that is pandemic throughout the West. In teaching the truth about marriage, about love, and about the complementarity of the sexes, the Catholic Church is proposing the path to happiness and human flourishing, not the road to repression and misery. The Synod ought to have made a bold, data-driven case in defense of that teaching, which is a defense of the dignity of the human person.

At the same time, the Synod debates suggested that the entire Church must engage in a much more serious discussion about the "ladder of love", an image for the spiritual life that Saint Augustine adopted from Plato's *Symposium*. At the Synod, it was suggested that, as a matter of pastoral strategy, the Church should approach people "where they are" on that ladder of love, no matter how low the rung. That is certainly true, and indeed always has been true. But the Church approaches people "where they are" on the ladder in order to invite them to climb higher, with the help of God's grace mediated through the Church's sacraments. Finding worthy elements in irregular marital situations or irregular sexual relationships is not a matter of endorsing those irregularities, but of inviting people to ascend the ladder. This means helping them understand the fullness of the good and encouraging them to seek it, with the help of grace. The challenge here is as old as Paul's efforts on the Areopagus, and it is not going to go away. But discussion of how to invite men and women to climb higher on the ladder of love will not be advanced by appeals to compassion that effectively detach compassion from truth, or by accommodating contemporary shibboleths about sexuality in any of its expressions.

One of the standard media tropes of Synod-2014 coverage, too often drawn from unfortunate comments by some Synod Fathers, was the difference between "doctrine" and "pastoral practice". The two are obviously not the same. But it is just as obvious that certain ecclesial practices, such as defining the conditions that constitute (or impede) worthiness to receive Holy Communion, are closely linked to settled doctrine, the doctrine, drawn from the Lord himself, that marriage is indissoluble (Mk 10:11–12), and the implication of that doctrine for the proper reception of Holy Communion, which is drawn from Saint Paul: "Whoever, therefore, eats the bread or drinks the cup of the Lord in an unworthy manner will be guilty of profaning the body and blood of the Lord" (1 Cor 11:27).

It was abundantly clear at Synod-2014 (to everyone except Cardinal Kasper, it seemed) that there was no consensus possible in favor of the Kasper proposals for changing the Church's practice in this matter, because doing so would constitute an impossible change in doctrine. Therefore, discussion should have focused on adjustments of the canonical processes by which marriages are judged null, and on the truths about the Holy Eucharist and the sacrament of penance that are at the root of the Church's settled understanding and practice concerning worthiness to receive Holy Communion. For all their faults—indeed *because* of their faults and the media attention they received—the Kasper proposals afford pastors and bishops a remarkable opportunity to recatechize (or, in many instances, catechize) their people about marriage, the Eucharist, and penance. Pastoral letters from bishops on these subjects can be helpful, but nothing is more important here than effective preaching.

Synod-2014's Final Report raised a strong protest about "pressure" being exerted on "the pastors of the Church" by cultural, political, and legal forces advancing the LGBT agenda, and rejected as "totally unacceptable" the machinations of "international organizations who link financial assistance to poorer countries with the introduction of laws which establish 'marriage' between persons of the same sex". That was useful pushback against the agenda of the U.S. Agency for International Development and the Obama State Department, among others. Discussion of these "pressures" ought to have afforded the Church's pastors another opportunity to clarify for the Church's people the essential difference between the sacramental covenant of marriage, on the one hand, and the civil contract of a private sexual relationship that is accorded public legal recognition by the state, on the other. That clarification should lead, in turn, to a thorough reexamination of the Church's relationship to civil marriage, centered on the question of how the Church might avoid complicity in the fraud of "same-sex marriage". Does the Church damage the credibility of its teaching within the household of faith, and weaken its witness in the public square, when Catholic deacons, priests, and bishops sign state marriage licenses that designate "Spouse 1" and "Spouse 2"? Such euphemisms signal an understanding of marriage that is not simply different from, but intrinsically opposed to, the Church's understanding. Discussions of the Church's relationship to civil marriage in a rapidly changing legal environment would also benefit by being framed within a richer ecclesiology than was often evident in the debates at Synod-2014, with the ancient concept of the family as the *ecclesiola*, the "little church", at the center of reflection on the relationship between the domestic church and the Mystical Body of Christ.

Finally, the Church's entire discussion of the crisis of marriage and the family in the twenty-first century should be more closely and explicitly linked to the New Evangelization. Men and women in the various marriage-preparation and campus ministries that have enjoyed real success in deploying the *Theology of the Body* and other postconciliar Catholic theological and pastoral developments to the challenging tasks of evangelization and catechesis in hostile cultural environments are a crucial resource for the Church's pastors. Their striking absence from Synod-2014 smacked of a new, progressive Catholic clericalism. Throughout the Church, this practical pastoral experience is a rich complement to the theoretical insights that faculty from the John Paul II Institutes on Marriage and the Family have been developing for two decades.

In his closing address to Synod-2014, Pope Francis underscored three concerns: a passionate concern for mission, a compassionate concern for people in difficult situations, and a committed concern for the settled truths of the Catholic faith. Holding those three concerns together was the challenge faced by Synod-2014. That challenge was not altogether successfully met. But the concerns remain.

# Synod-2015

## *What Really Happened, Why, and How*

When the Fourteenth Ordinary General Assembly of the Synod of Bishops opened with a concelebrated Mass at the Altar of the Confession in Saint Peter's Basilica on October 4, 2015, it was already clear that there would be three Synods: the real Synod, the mainstream media Synod, and the blogosphere Synod. The first and third would be daily affairs; the second would be more sporadic. Both participants and observers wondered what effect the second and third would have on the first.

As things turned out, the short answer to that initial puzzlement was "not much", except by way of providing occasional amusement and aggravation. As always, the mainstream media kept looking for confirmation of its perception of Pope Francis as the long-awaited papal reformer who would adjust Catholic doctrine and practice to the *Zeitgeist*, especially in terms of the sexual revolution. The blogosphere, dependent on the mainstream media for what it foolishly regarded as accurate information, was largely divided between those who enthusiastically shared these hopes for a Franciscan revolution of a liberal Protestant sort, and those who were scared to death that the enthusiasts were right about the Pope from the ends of the earth. So for three weeks the media Synod and the blogosphere Synod followed their own prepackaged scripts and were not very interesting as a result.

The actual Synod, however, was another matter.

Real issues were debated, with real consequences at stake. Some of this was visible beneath the froth of the mainstream media and blogosphere commentary. How would the Catholic Church settle the argument, launched by Cardinal Walter Kasper in February 2014, about its long-standing and doctrinally informed discipline of not admitting the divorced and civilly remarried to Holy Communion? And beneath that debate, other and deeper issues loomed.

Perhaps the most fundamental involved the claims of revelation on the pastoral life of the Church. Did the Catholic Church still affirm the Second Vatican Council's teaching in the Dogmatic Constitution on Divine Revelation, *Dei Verbum*, that revelation is both real and binding? How was revelation to be related to the signs of the times, which the Church was enjoined to read by Vatican II's Pastoral Constitution on the Church in the Modern World, *Gaudium et Spes*? And how did all of that bear on the relationship between mercy and truth, between pastoral accompaniment and pastoral challenge, between one's condition of life and one's ability to receive the grace of the sacraments?

The fact that, for the first time in two thousand years, the Catholic Church is "catholic" (universal, global) in an existential sense put other important questions in play. How should the experience of the young churches of Africa, where the Christian idea of marriage and family is received as a liberating force, be weighed against the experience of dying churches in which divorce is more common than Sunday Mass attendance, local churches whose leaders claimed before the Synod that Catholicism's teaching on divorce drives people away from God?

Then there were the issues posed by that ancient malady known as *odium theologicum*. Some Synod Fathers came to Synod-2015, as they had come to its preparatory predecessor, Synod-2014, determined to re-adjudicate Paul VI's 1968 encyclical on the morally appropriate means of regulating fertility (*Humanae Vitae*) and John Paul II's 1993 encyclical on the reform of Catholic moral theology (*Veritatis Splendor*). Those who wished to bury those two encyclicals were, in the main, identical with those pressing the Kasper proposal for admitting the divorced and civilly remarried to Holy Communion. Those who found the Kasper proposal woefully deficient on many grounds were, in the main, those who judged that *Humanae Vitae* had been prophetic in its analysis of what a "contraceptive mentality" would do to Western culture and society; who thought that *Veritatis Splendor* had rescued Catholic moral theology from the quicksand of postmodern subjectivism; and who believed that the "signs of the times" (pace *Gaudium et Spes*) should be read *through* the lens of divine revelation (pace *Dei Verbum*), rather than taken as the principal hermeneutic tool for understanding revelation today.

The contest over the Catholic Church's response to the sexual revolution, which involves basic questions of the Church's self-understanding and the Church's pastoral approach to mission, will of course continue long past Synod-2015. Nonetheless, the arguments abroad in Rome during that meeting, and the way the great majority of them were resolved in the Synod's Final Report, reinforced the doctrinal and theological foundations on which that contest must be fought, claims to the contrary from those who lost most of what they were seeking in Rome notwithstanding. Yet the debate and the confusions in pastoral practice engendered by Pope Francis' ambiguous post-synodal apostolic exhortation, *Amoris Laetitia* (The Joy of Love), demonstrated that the losers at Synod-2014 and Synod-2015 refused to concede defeat.

To put all of that into clearer focus, and to see just how the ambiguities of *Amoris Laetitia* run contrary to the consensus of Synod-2015 even as the exhortation's marvelous passages reflect the Synod's work and the Synod Fathers' agreements, it's helpful to review what actually happened in Rome during October 2015.

Long before the Synod Fathers began assembling in Rome, it was clear that many of them were deeply concerned about the working document (the *Instrumentum Laboris*) they had been given. In the months after it was made available in the summer of 2015, the *Instrumentum Laboris* was severely criticized for numerous deficiencies. The first had to do with structure: Why did an ecclesial document begin with sociology (and not very good sociology) rather than the Word of God? Shouldn't the latter be the first thing reflected upon, so that the kaleidoscopic crisis of marriage and the family today would come into a sharper and appropriately Christian focus?

Many Synod Fathers also found the language of the *Instrumentum Laboris* dull and uninspired, as if the Church, confronted with the cultural tsunami of the sexual revolution, had run out of intellectual gas and pastoral nerve and was mildly embarrassed by its teaching—especially the teaching of *Veritatis Splendor* and John Paul II's *Theology of the Body*, neither of which was prominently featured (to put it gently) in the *Instrumentum Laboris*. There were also thought to be dangerous ambiguities in the *Instrumentum Laboris'* discussion of pastoral practice; on that front, more than a few episcopal eyebrows were raised by the fact that the Synod general secretariat had ignored its own ground rules by inserting into the working document for Synod-2015 material that was not in the Final Report of Synod-2014.

In the forty-eight hours before the Synod began its work, however, these concerns were superseded by grave concerns over synodal process. With two days to go, it was unclear whether there would be *any* votes on *anything* at the Synod—which would have been an unprecedented change in procedure, for votes on propositions had always been the way the Synod Fathers made their judgments known to the Church and the world. Moreover, the Fathers were informed that their interventions in the Synod's general assembly would be the Synod's property and would not be made public. (The less-than-persuasive rationale offered for this by the Synod general secretary, Cardinal Lorenzo Baldisseri, was that this would foster more open debate.)

Beyond that, it seemed that the reports from the Synod's thirteen language-based discussion groups, where the serious discussions would unfold, were not going to be made public, either. And beyond even that, many believed that the drafting commission announced by Cardinal Baldisseri to prepare the Synod's Final Report (the publication of which was also in doubt) was badly skewed and did not reflect the balance of opinion among the Synod Fathers.

This was simply unacceptable to a large number of bishops, who were not eager to spend three weeks locked down in a virtual cone of silence from which nothing would emerge, a lockdown that treated them as appendages to the Synod general secretariat and enmeshed them in a secretive process that would cause the deepest suspicions in the Church and the world about what was afoot. These concerns found expression in a private letter to Pope Francis that was given to him at the end of the Synod's first working day (Monday, October 5) and which was signed by thirteen cardinals, including three prefects of major dicasteries of the Roman Curia and ten residential archbishops from four continents.

Because the letter was a private one to the Vicar of Christ, its signatories did not believe that its contents should be made public, even after an early draft of the letter was leaked. But it can be stated as a matter of fact that the letter was entirely respectful of the Pope's person and prerogatives; that it expressed the cardinals' concern that the Pope's call for an open and frank conversation was going to be impeded by the proposed Synod process; that it requested a normal voting procedure so that the Fathers could make their judgments known; that it sought greater openness in making available to the Church and the world the participants' reflections in both the general assembly and the language-based discussion groups; and that it looked forward to a Final Report prepared so as to reflect the entire Synod.

Two days later, most of the letter's requests had been honored. The general secretary announced that the Synod Fathers could, if they wished, make their general assembly interventions available to the press and to their dioceses. The reports of the language-based discussion groups would be made public. There would be votes on the draft of the Final Report, paragraph by paragraph. The disposition of this *Relatio Finalis* remained the prerogative of the Pope, as was entirely proper, but it was assumed that the report would be made public. (Veterans of the Vatican naturally assumed that it would be leaked within twenty-four hours of its completion, in any event.)

If the cardinals' letter transformed the process, the introduction to the *Instrumentum Laboris* on the first working day by the Synod's Hungarian *relator* (rapporteur-general), Cardinal Péter Erdő, was the substantive game-changer. It was anticipated that Cardinal Erdő would give three introductions, one to each of the *Instrumentum Laboris'* three parts, at the beginning of each week's work. Erdő chose instead to offer an introduction to the entire working document on the first day of the Synod. In doing so, he set a solid foundation for the Synod's deliberations that effectively corrected the gross inadequacies of the *Instrumentum Laboris* (which by this point had been conceded by virtually everyone except the German-speaking participants and the general secretariat, which had authored it).

Cardinal Erdő began by putting the Synod on a firm ecclesial footing, describing marriage and family life as *vocations*—institutions given by God as part of the "divine pedagogy" in which we learn the dignity of human life and human love, and the true meaning of our being made male and female. The Hungarian cardinal then looked at marriage and the family through the prism of revelation and doctrine, noting that, in the Creator's design, the unitive and

procreative dimensions of marriage were "inscribed" as truths built
into us. Christ's work of redemption, he continued, had restored
within marriage and the family "the image of the Most Holy Trinity,
from which springs every true love".

Cardinal Erdő also located the Christian family in the context
of John Paul II's New Evangelization and Pope Francis' call for a
"Church permanently in mission", reminding the Synod Fathers that
"the missionary dimension of the family is rooted in the sacrament
of Baptism, through which all are commissioned to be missionary
disciples", and from which the Christian family is constituted as a
"domestic Church". That was why the family, as Saint John Paul
had taught in the 1981 apostolic exhortation *Familiaris Consortio*, is
the way of the Church—a point Blessed Paul VI had underscored
in the encyclical *Humanae Vitae*, when he noted the many ways in
which modern technology detached marriage from family by separating procreation from conjugal love. Moreover, as Benedict XVI had
written in the encyclical *Caritas in Veritate*, the experience of love in
marriage and the family is vital to the life of society because the family is the place where one learns the meaning of the common good
through experience.

The rapporteur-general underscored that the "teaching of Christ
on matrimony" (i.e., monogamy and the indissolubility of marriage)
was a "true gospel and a font of joy" in which the human person
realizes his or her "vocation to personal relationships" of freedom,
mutual self-gift, and full acceptance of the other. The teaching on
indissolubility, the cardinal noted, comes from the Gospels and Saint
Paul, and has always distinguished the Christian view of marriage
from others'.

Thus, in the first half hour of his talk, Erdő set the discussions
of Synod-2015 on a solid foundation built from the Scriptures and
the magisterium of the three preceding pontificates, thereby tacitly
rejecting the false premise that the Fathers could start from scratch
in considering marriage and the family in the twenty-first century.
The signs of the times, he concurrently made clear, should be read
through the lens of divine revelation.

But the Hungarian prelate wasn't done yet.

Cardinal Erdő reminded the Synod Fathers that mercy and revealed
truth cannot be opposed, for "merciful love, as it attracts and unites,

also transforms and lifts up. It is an invitation to conversion." In this light, "a merciful pastoral accompaniment of the divorced and civilly remarried" cannot "leave in doubt" the "truth of the indissolubility of marriage taught by Jesus Christ himself." "The mercy of God," he continued, "offers sinners pardon" but always "calls to conversion".

Erdő then criticized one of the arguments being offered in favor of the Kasper proposal to admit the divorced and civilly remarried to Holy Communion at the end of a "penitential path", but without a judgment of nullity about the first marriage. As Erdő put it, "it is not the shipwreck of the first marriage but the living-together in the second relationship that impedes access to the Eucharist." The cardinal then pointed out a possible way forward, citing the teaching of John Paul II in *Familiaris Consortio* (no. 84): when those who in conscience believe that, for the sake of their children or the common life they have built in a second marriage, they must remain in that marriage, there is access to the sacraments of penance and the Eucharist when the couple practices continence, "living their relationship as one of mutual help and friendship". Such a requirement on the part of the Church does not, Erdő said, reduce marriage to a mere exercise in sexual expression. Rather, it recognizes the reality of the situation in light of the truth about marriage taught by Christ. There is, in other words, a true path to the sacraments for the divorced and civilly remarried and there always had been: the path of continence.

As to the question of "gradualism" in an individual's or couple's growth in the moral life, a concept often used as a side step into the Kasper proposal, Cardinal Erdő said that, while we all grow in the life of grace, "between true and false, between good and evil, there is in fact no such 'graduality' ". And although there may be "some positive aspects" to be found in irregular relationships, "this does not imply" that these relationships "can be presented as good".

Cardinal Erdő then turned to an issue many thought would be the next step beyond the Kasper proposal: a tacit ecclesial blessing on homosexual unions. While urging respect and sensitive pastoral care for people who experience same-sex attraction, he stated flatly that "there is no foundation" in truth for making any "analogy, however remote, between homosexual unions and God's design for marriage and the family". The cardinal also urged the pastors of the Church to resist campaigns to affirm these new designs for building families, and stated bluntly that the pressures put on poor countries by international institutions that condition financial aid on the former's acceptance of same-sex marriage were "unacceptable".

The rapporteur-general's conclusion urged the Synod Fathers to continue their attentive listening to the Word of God so that the Church's response "to the needs of our contemporaries" may be one that "offers them liberating truth" in the witness of greater mercy. For his labors, the Hungarian prelate received a warm ovation; Cardinal Kasper, who reportedly looked somewhat stunned, was not among those applauding.

Cardinal Erdő's decision to treat the entire subject matter of the Synod at the outset effectively buried the *Instrumentum Laboris* as Synod-2015's guiding document. The general assembly and small-group discussions would continue to work from the tripartite structure of the *Instrumentum Laboris*, but Erdő's introductory intervention had the happy effect of liberating the Synod participants.

Rather than slavishly following the deeply flawed *Instrumentum Laboris*, they could now probe far more deeply into the Christian tradition, and into the contemporary situation of marriage and the family, which includes good news as well as bad, in order to develop and reform the Church's pastoral response to a profound cultural and human crisis. Moreover, the Hungarian cardinal's talk took any possible endorsement of civil unions among same-sex couples off the table while putting paid to the Kasper proposal in its initial form. And while Kasper's allies would not throw in the towel, at the end of the Synod's first day it was much more likely that Synod-2015 would not repeat the experience of Synod-2014 and be hijacked by the preoccupations of the German-speaking fathers.

While the Kasper proposal in its initial form was effectively derailed by Cardinal Erdő's introductory intervention, its proponents were nothing if not tenacious. Thus the proposal reappeared in new forms, each of which provoked important debates on deeper issues in the general assembly and in the language-based discussion groups. In each of these guises, proponents continued to claim that the whole matter of Holy Communion for the divorced and civilly remarried was not about a "change in doctrine" (which the Pope had insisted was untouchable) but a "change in discipline" or a "change in pastoral practice". That dodge got very little traction, however, not least because it was asserted rather than argued, and in any event had been thoroughly vetted (and rejected) in the run-up to Synod-2014 and in the year between the Synods. So the Kasper party (largely, it should be noted, without the active participation of Cardinal Kasper, who was strikingly quiet) deployed other stratagems. And in doing so, the Kasperites ironically, and almost certainly unintentionally, contributed to a deepening of the meeting's debates and of the Church's understanding of the issues beneath the issues at Synod-2015.

The Kasperites' Plan B was a variant on the Febronianism that plagued German-speaking Catholicism throughout the Enlightenment and was quickly dubbed "local-option Catholicism", a useful tag that was widely adopted. In essence, Plan B asked the Church to reconceive itself as a federation of national churches, united symbolically by the successor of Peter, but substantially independent of each other (and Rome) doctrinally and pastorally. Thus national or continental bishops' conferences would be empowered to find local "solutions" to the challenges posed by the contemporary crisis of marriage and the family.

No one paying attention had any doubt about the direction such a devolution would take in certain quarters.

In Germany, Austria, Switzerland, and Belgium, for example, the practice of offering Holy Communion to the divorced and civilly remarried was already widespread, and what was being sought was a means of affirming what was already happening (or, in the spin put on this by some German speakers, giving the bishops a tool by which the episcopal conferences in question could get some control over the practice by establishing criteria for it).

In response, Synod Fathers from around the world pointed out the unhappy role that local-option ecclesiology has had in fragmenting the Anglican Communion to the point of virtual disintegration. The even sharper theological case against the Kasperites' Plan B was put forward by the Synod Fathers who argued from basic sacramental logic: it simply cannot be the case that what is sacrilege in Poland is a font of grace on the other side of the Polish-German border. That argument eventually carried the day, and another important marker was laid down: a decisive majority of the Synod Fathers were determined that the Catholic Church would remain one, in both doctrine and sacramental discipline.

With Plan A and Plan B off the board, Plan C was deployed, in the form of an appeal to the rights of conscience. Surely, the dogged Kasperites argued, the final arbiter of the decision on worthiness to receive Holy Communion is the individual, confronting his or her situation in the sanctuary of conscience, acknowledged as inviolable by Vatican II in its Declaration on Religious Freedom, *Dignitatis Humanae*. Critics quickly pointed out, however, that the Catholic Church (and *Dignitatis Humanae*) had never considered "conscience" a free-floating faculty of choice detached from religious and moral truth. It was true, Cardinal Thomas Collins of Toronto and others argued, that the *Catechism of the Catholic Church* teaches the imperative of obeying one's conscience. But it also reminds the faithful of the imperative of having a rightly formed conscience. And the duty of the twenty-first-century pastors of the Church was, surely, to call the people of the Church beyond the expressive individualism that has reduced human beings to bundles of desires (vitiating the idea of "conscience" in the process).

The Church, these Synod Fathers argued, had ample resources with which to propose a richer understanding of the nobility of human choosing and the human capacity, under grace, to choose wisely and well, even in difficult circumstances, and it ought to deploy them more effectively. Blessed John Henry Newman's *Letter to the Duke of Norfolk* was cited to good effect in these debates. Then Plan C was given the coup de grâce by a five-minute, six-point explication of the Catholic understanding of conscience by Cardinal Carlo Caffarra of Bologna, in a strikingly lucid general assembly intervention that was being discussed with reverence days after it was given.

The Germans being nothing if not persistent, it came down, in the end, to Plan D: decisions on "pastoral accompaniment" of the divorced and civilly remarried should be made in the "internal forum" by a penitent and confessor. Some described this as "local-option Catholicism" taken all the way down to the parish level, a farm-to-table version of sacramental theology. Other Synod Fathers, less theologically alert, seemed to find in Plan D a way to be compassionate without abandoning essential Catholic doctrine—and perhaps a "solution" by which to mollify the German speakers, who were, in the main, having a bad Synod. As things finally resolved themselves, the phrase "internal forum" did make it into the Synod's Final Report. But it was circumscribed in a way that the proponents of Plan D obviously found disturbing, because they denied that any such hedging-about had taken place.

While these real debates about real issues were unfolding in the Synod Hall and the language-based discussion groups, the world media were having fits, in large part because there was no story to cover. The debates took place behind closed doors. Some bishops shared their general assembly interventions with the press, but for the most part, the gathered scribes had little to do until the discussion groups' reports began to be released days after the Synod opened. Thus the press was reduced to what the *Boston Globe*'s John Allen accurately described as reporting on what others said was happening in the Synod (or even reporting on reporting on what others said was happening at the Synod), rather than reporting on what was actually happening.

This led to the usual fantasies and distortions in the Italian media, which too many gullible Anglophone journalists take seriously and then refract, undistilled, into the Anglosphere. But as usual during large-scale Catholic events at the Vatican, the Italian press had more than its elbow up its sleeve, and there was a lot more going on in Italian coverage of the Synod than coverage of the Synod. There was pre-conclave politicking, inevitable with a Pope about to turn seventy-nine. And then there was the traditional score-settling and agenda-agitating, these not infrequently involving the financial reforms that Cardinal George Pell had put in place since 2014.

That Pell was a leader among the challengers to the Kasper proposal in its sundry iterations afforded the Australian cardinal's critics and enemies an opportunity: use the Synod debates as a blind behind which to take potshots at him, suggesting that he was disrespectful of the Pope or even disloyal to the man who had appointed him to clean out the Augean stables of Vatican finance. The goal was to whittle down Pell, a large figure in every way, to the point where his further excavations into the darker corners of financial incompetence (and worse) in the Holy See would be impeded and perhaps even halted, thus sparing embarrassment (and worse) to favored leakers, patrons, or both.

These two dynamics—the lack of news and Italianate journalists' game-playing to protect favored Vatican sources—came together in the most hilariously off-base piece written during Synod-2015. The article, by Paolo Rodari, sprawled over two pages of the October 14, 2015, issue of *La Repubblica* and set a new standard for fantasy wedded to malice.

Pell was cast as one of the leading figures in a plot by the *"Rigoristi"* to block Pope Francis' pastoral initiatives, the other principal villains being Cardinals Gerhard Müller of the Congregation for the Doctrine of the Faith; Timothy Dolan of New York; Robert Sarah of the Congregation for Divine Worship; Wilfred Napier of Durban, South Africa; and the aforementioned Carlo Caffarra. The plot, Rodari wrote, was headquartered at the Pontifical North American College, was financed by the Knights of Columbus, and had ominous links to former vice president Dick Cheney, Halliburton, and the American Enterprise Institute—and through Cheney's wife, Lynne, to the merchants of death at Lockheed Martin. Opposing this unholy cabal were the *"Progressisti"*. And here, Paolo Rodari's fevered imagination went further into overdrive. For alongside such obvious champions of "progress" as Cardinals Walter Kasper, Reinhard Marx, and Godfried Danneels, Rodari included Archbishop Charles Chaput of Philadelphia, who was being lambasted almost daily in the progressive U.S. Catholic press and blogosphere, for whom he embodies the antithesis of everything "progressive".

Chaput was vindicated ten days later, when he received one of the highest numbers of votes for election to the Synod's permanent council. Paolo Rodari and *La Repubblica*, for their part, gave Synod participants and knowledgeable observers some good laughs, even as this intermezzo of serious craziness further illustrated a basic tenet of Vaticanology 101: there is no fixed border between fact and fiction in Italian journalism but only a membrane across which all sorts of material, some of it in the form of waste, flows.

The Synod Fathers were given the draft of the Final Report on the afternoon of Thursday, October 22 (the liturgical memorial of Saint John Paul II). The draft was available in Italian only. And thanks to a change of schedule that could be plausibly interpreted as an attempt to constrain the Fathers' ability to mount serious criticisms of the draft, the Synod's members had only twelve hours to study the draft, decide what comments they wished to make on it at the general assembly on Friday morning, October 23, and formulate the *modi* (amendments) they would submit in writing that morning. Then, the drafting committee was to get back to work Friday afternoon to prepare the amended text that would be voted on, paragraph by paragraph, on Saturday.

Despite the truncated schedule, more than a few Synod Fathers were pleasantly surprised by the draft they received on October 22. The *Instrumentum Laboris* had been essentially jettisoned as the basis for the Final Report, and the draft was far richer biblically, and far more elegantly written, than anything that had previously issued from the Synod general secretariat (which led to speculations about its real authorship, the drafting committee being more or less in the pocket of the Synod general secretariat). Be that as it may, one Synod Father went so far as to observe Thursday night that, had the draft Final Report been the Synod's working document, the whole process would have been far more intellectually satisfying, and far more conducive to fostering the kind of discussion for which the Pope had called.

But there were problems, and they centered around three paragraphs in the draft Final Report: 84, 85, and 86. Interventions were sketched out and more than two dozen *modi* were prepared to remedy the perceived ambiguities in language on the nature and direction of pastoral care of the divorced and civilly remarried. Given the lateness of the hour, so to speak, many of the *modi* submitted Friday morning, and more than twenty oral interventions on Friday, proposed dropping one, two, or all three of the unsatisfactory paragraphs, rather than attempting to amend them. An effort was also made to have the Final Report quote the crucial paragraph number 84 of *Familiaris Consortio* in full, rather than in bowdlerized form.

In the event, those interventions and *modi* were largely ignored, with one crucial exception. The revised draft on which the Synod Fathers voted Saturday afternoon anchored paragraph 85's discussion of the "internal forum" in the Church's tradition: such pastoral discernment between penitent and priest was to be undertaken "according to the teaching of the Church", a phrase inserted between the Friday debates and the Saturday vote. Some Fathers nonetheless regarded the paragraph as insufficiently precise and came within a handful of votes of denying it the two-thirds approval needed for inclusion in the Final Report.

Imperfections and ambiguities notwithstanding, the Final Report was a massive improvement over the *Instrumentum Laboris*, and illustrated just how significantly the thirteen cardinals' letter, Erdő's introductory intervention, and the debates in the general assembly and the language groups had changed both the dynamics and the content of Synod–2015.

The Final Report was an unmistakably ecclesial text, a product of the Church's meditation on the Word of God, understood as the lens through which the Church interprets the signs of the times. And while the working document was biblically anorexic, the Final Report was richly, even eloquently, biblical, thereby vindicating *Dei Verbum* a few weeks before the fiftieth anniversary of its promulgation.

The working document's seeming embarrassment over Catholic teaching on chastity, fidelity, and worthiness to receive Holy Communion was replaced by an impressive reaffirmation of the possibility of living virtuously in the postmodern world. At the same time, the report called the Church to a more effective proclamation of the truths it bears as a patrimony from the Lord Jesus himself, and to more solicitous pastoral care of those in difficult marital and familial circumstances.

Children were largely missing from the *Instrumentum Laboris*. By contrast, the Final Report described children as a great blessing, praised large families, was careful to honor children with special needs, and lifted up the witness of happily and fruitfully married couples and their kids as agents of evangelization.

The working document's confused discussion of conscience was replaced by a far more serious explication of the Church's understanding of conscience's relationship to truth, as the Final Report rejected the idea that the "inviolability" of conscience amounts to a moral "Get Out of Jail Free" card.

The working document was full of ambiguities about the relationship of pastoral practice to doctrine. The Final Report made clear that these two realities are closely linked in the life of the Catholic Church. Authentic pastoral care must begin from a commitment to the settled teaching of the Church, and there is no such thing as "local-option Catholicism".

The working document was also ambiguous in describing the "family". The Final Report underscored that there can be no proper analogy drawn between the Catholic understanding of "marriage" and "family" and other social arrangements, no matter what their legal status.

Mercy and truth were sometimes put in tension in the working document. The Final Report was far more theologically developed in relating mercy and truth in God, which means that mercy and truth are inseparable in the doctrine and practice of the Church.

In sum, the Final Report of Synod-2015, though not without flaws, went a very long way (and light years beyond the *Instrumentum Laboris*) in lifting up and celebrating the Catholic vision of marriage and the family as a luminous answer to the crisis of those institutions in the twenty-first century. And, claims to the contrary notwithstanding, the Final Report said not a single word about admitting the divorced and civilly remarried to Holy Communion, absent a decree of nullity.

The election of Archbishop Chaput and Cardinals Pell, Sarah, Napier, and Marc Ouellet to the Synod's permanent council ensured that there would be strong voices pressing for an improved Synod process in the future. Virtually everyone except Cardinal Baldisseri and his fellow Synod managers agreed, for example, that there should be real exchange and debate in the general assemblies, which requires immediate translation of interventions and texts into the major world languages. Moreover, the Fourteenth Ordinary General Assembly of the Synod of Bishops underscore a point previously demonstrated at Synod-2014: that the representatives of the national bishops' conferences will not be treated as schoolchildren by the Synod managers, who are their servants, not their masters. These seemed positive developments for the future of "synodality" in the Catholic Church. Nevertheless, Synod-2015 also revealed fault lines in the Church that could no longer be denied.

The Synod also underlined what has been known, if rarely spoken of publicly, for some years: much of the Church in northern Europe is in a de facto state of schism, not formally detached from Rome and the rest of the world Church, but thinking and living its own ecclesial reality. Some northern European bishops manifestly do not believe and teach what the Catholic Church believes and teaches. German ecclesiology at the ground level is in such a shambles that those who decline to pay the state-collected *Kirchensteuer* (church tax) can be denied Holy Communion and access to the other sacraments, while those living in irregular relationships are regularly offered Holy Communion. Addressing this de facto (but not de jure) separation of northern European Catholicism from the unity of the world Church—a sad by-product of intellectual confusions and intellectual arrogance leading to massive pastoral failure—is a serious issue for the Catholic future.

The experience of Synod-2015 also suggested that too many of the Church's bishops have a tenuous grasp on doctrine and a palpable disinclination to discuss grave pastoral matters in their appropriately theological context. Pastorally skillful bishops are, obviously, an imperative. But the early twenty-first century is a moment of cultural crisis in the West. Bad ideas underwrite ideologies that make war on human nature, especially male-female complementarity, and deconstruct the basic norms and institutions that promote human flourishing (often deploying coercive state power to accelerate the deconstruction). Surely the Church can find pastorally skilled and humanly compelling men who can meet the challenge of those desperately deficient ideas, which are magnifying the sum total of human unhappiness: intellectually sophisticated pastors who can invite the walking wounded of postmodernity to the joy of conversion.

Synod-2015 also demonstrated that the American Catholic experience of the past three decades is still not sufficiently "in play" in the deliberations of the world Church. There are a lot of things wrong with Catholicism in the United States. But the Church in the United States has learned some things about deploying resources such as *Familiaris Consortio* and the *Theology of the Body* in catechesis and marriage preparation that remain wholly unlearned, it seems, in other local churches in Europe and Latin America. Some of what has been learned in these pastoral and catechetical successes was put in play at Synod-2015; much more could be done in future gatherings of this sort.

The evangelical task of the Church continues, of course, irrespective of what happens at Synods. Had it gone a different way, Synod-2015 might have seriously impeded that work in the liveliest and most vital parts of the world Church. But the Synod reaffirmed the Gospel and the settled truths of Catholic faith and practice. Those who are doing the work of the New Evangelization took encouragement from that and got on with living the missionary discipleship to which they were called in baptism. That work continued, even after Pope Francis' apostolic exhortation concluding the work of the Synod, *Amoris Laetitia*, and the wildly varying responses to it, reopened and intensified the very arguments that the majority of the Synod Fathers thought they had resolved in October 2014 and October 2015.

# Evangelical Churchmanship

## *Learning from an Earlier Francis*

When Sir Kenneth Clark devoted an episode to the Middle Ages in his magisterial BBC series, *Civilisation*, he began by celebrating the chivalry, courtesy, and romance of the French and Burgundian courts—the Gothic world of "imaginative fancy" that coexisted with a "sharp sense of reality". Clark no doubt surprised some of his viewers by then launching into an encomium to a medieval, chivalric figure of a quite distinctive sort, the spiritual knight errant who, by the time of his death, had captured the imagination of much of Europe: Saint Francis of Assisi.

He was a man of sanctity, but there were others before him. What made Saint Francis so influential was his extraordinary originality: the son of a rich businessman who renounced his wealth and slept in pigsties while retaining the courtliness and gentility that were noble attributes of his era; the antiestablishment figure who founded a great religious institution; the man of radical poverty whose followers were not permitted (even if they had wanted) to imitate his utter rejection of worldly goods; the man of the Bible who never owned a complete one; the author of the first great literary work in Italian dialect, the "Canticle of the Sun", who was steeped in the *jongleur* tradition of French poetry and song; the naïf who moved the heart and enriched the religious imagination of that great realist and exponent of papal power, Innocent III; the child of the age of Crusades who sought not the conquest of the Muslims but their conversion—and so forth and so on, almost, if not quite, *per omnia saecula saeculorum*.

His enduring magnetism, which is bound up with the paradoxes of his life, has led to many "false Francises". Marxists claimed him as a medieval anticipation of their project. It was probably inevitable that, during the Sixties, hippies found in Francis an anticipation of Haight-Ashbury and Woodstock, dropping out and turning on. Contemporary environmentalists transform Francis' biblical piety about God's creation into a prototype of their worship of a quite different god, Gaia. An immense body of scholarship on the life, thought, and impact of Saint Francis ably refutes these distortions. But then came the first pope to take as his regnal title the name of one of Catholicism's most popular saints, and the reinvention of Francesco Bernardone has started all over again—this time, in the form of projecting onto Saint Francis what observers admire in his papal namesake.

Francis-reinventing is unfortunate, but not simply because it distorts the historical record. The real Saint Francis of Assisi has much to teach the Catholic Church in the turbulent twenty-first century. And perhaps the first and foremost lesson to be learned from him is how to be truly men and women *of* the Church. For, notwithstanding his originality and, by some lights, eccentricity, Francesco Bernardone was always and profoundly an obedient (if not always docile) son of the Catholic Church.

His deep ecclesial sensibility, so at odds with the autonomy project that warps both Church and culture today, is nicely captured in an incident from his life. It seems that the *Poverello*, the "little poor one", was traveling in Lombardy and stopped in a church to pray. A local Manichean—Italy really was full of strange and wondrous characters in those days—wanted to use Francis to draw some villagers to his sect. The local pastor was living with a concubine, and the Manichean, seeking to exploit the scandal, asked Francis, "If the priest maintains a concubine and stains his hands, must one put faith in his teaching and respect the sacraments he administers?" Francis, understanding the game being played, went down on his knees before the wayward priest and the local people, and replied:

> I do not know if these hands are really stained as the other claims. What I do know, in any case, is that, even if they were, that would not in any way diminish the power and efficacy of the sacraments of God. These hands remain the channel through which the grace and benefits of God stream toward the people. That is why I kiss them, out of respect for the one who delegated his authority to them.

Francis knew, and we should know, that God took a risk on the Church. That risk was to put the means and instruments of beatitude and salvation into human hands, into the hands of sinners who would make a mess of things from time to time. But as Francis understood the economy of salvation and the radical obedience to which the disciples of the Lord Jesus are called, if God saw fit to take a risk on the humanity of the Church, who are we to deem that a mistake? At the same time, Francis was a genuine reformer who called the comfortable religious professionals of his time to a life beyond clericalism and privilege. Rather than staying becalmed in the sacristy, the sanctuary, and the presbytery, the clergy of his day, he urged, should lead a demanding, Gospel-centered life of proclaiming the Word and celebrating the sacraments, nourishing their people with the tangible realities God had entrusted to human hands as pathways to the Trinity: the Bible and the Eucharist.

Saint Francis' churchmanship, if we may call it that, was closely related to his radically incarnational religious imagination, which is his second important legacy to our times, beset as we are by new forms of Gnosticism. That Francis and his first companions made a fuss over the restoration of abandoned churches and the cleaning of ill-kept churches was not simply because the *Poverello* had dreams in which he was told to rebuild churches; those dreams and that work had a deeper meaning. Rebuilding fallen walls, sweeping dirty church floors, and cleaning ill-kept sacred vessels were expressions, however simple, of the profoundly incarnational conviction that animated Francis' life and mission. It was the conviction that, because of the Incarnation, what lies between the ordinary and the extraordinary is not a border, and still less a wall, but something rather more like a porous, diaphanous veil, through which spiritual riches flow in abundance. The Incarnate Word conscripts the tangibilities of ecclesial life, and even creation itself, to draw us into the divine life.

In our Gnostic culture, which devalues the givenness of things and the revelatory power built into that givenness, this Franciscan reminder to twenty-first-century Christians is of crucial importance. It is through material things—water, salt, and oil; bread and wine; marital love—that the Father of our Lord Jesus Christ comes to the people the Son has made his own. This radical incarnationalism has considerable pastoral and apologetic implications. If two millennia of argument have not finished off Gnosticism, that most protean of heresies, it seems unlikely that contemporary arguments, no matter how persuasive orthodox believers may find them, will do the job with the unconverted, the skeptical, or the hostile. Thus the "incarnational" counter to contemporary Gnosticism and its ideology of "you are what you say you are" (irrespective, for example, of biology) will be less an argument than a demonstration: living in concord with the moral truths built into the world and into us, which lead to beatitude or happiness.

Arguments are important and Christians should keep making them. But in a postmodern world that can only concede "your truth" and "my truth" (before it tries to deploy coercive state power to impose *its* truth on everyone), it will be the witness of Christian lives that changes hearts and minds. This is especially true when Christians live nobly, courageously, and compassionately in service to those who have been most deeply wounded by the Gnostic cultural tsunami and its personally lethal effects. The days when an Evelyn Waugh could think his way into Catholicism with the help of a skilled Jesuit dialectician like Father Martin D'Arcy are over; our culture is too intellectually shattered for that to be the evangelical paradigm. The new paradigm must be in the Franciscan mode, with embodied witness coming first. Because of that witness, those who have been touched by Christian compassion or Christian nobility or Christian courage may be moved to ask, "How can you live this way?" And at that point, the door to the offer of friendship with Christ has been opened.

This incarnationalism leads, in turn, to the third Franciscan lesson for our time: Christian witness must be based on the experience of being saved by the radical self-emptying of Jesus Christ, who is Savior, not just moral exemplar. Francis, whose entire religious life sprang from a profound consciousness of having been saved, reminds us that *salvation* is at the heart of the Christian proclamation. Christianity is not about me, nor is it about feeling good about me. It's about salvation: rescue from all the self-induced afflictions to which humanity is prone; forgiveness when those afflictions overcome us; ultimately, life within the embrace of the Thrice-Holy God. A Franciscan renewal of twenty-first-century Catholicism will, of course, emphasize the works of charity and mercy as the entry point for evangelization. But that does not and cannot make the Church into another nongovernmental organization in the good-works business. The Church is about salvation or she is a fraud: a soup kitchen with smells and bells.

Francis, whose asceticism was exceptionally severe, could be a man of overflowing joy because he lived his adult life in the confidence that his salvation came not through his own merits, but from the superabundance of divine love manifest in Jesus Christ. That conviction was born from a profound spiritual experience that touched his heart and mind, his emotions as well as his intellect, so he wanted others to have a similar experience. Hence the crèche and its tender evocation of Christ's birth and infancy. Hence the evocative poetry, so redolent of a medieval troubadour celebrating his lady, which for Francis was Lady Poverty. And hence, ultimately, the stigmata. The God-given dignity squandered in the Garden of Eden had been restored at Easter to men and women who could now be, again, sons and daughters of the Most High God, and thus truly themselves; yet the path to Easter, Francis knew, went up the rocky hill of Calvary.

This is the *Poverello* at his most Pauline and Trinitarian. It is in the *kenosis*, the self-emptying, of the Son that the Father effects salvation in the power of the Spirit. In that sense, Francis of Assisi's life as a mendicant embodied in evangelical witness the truth of the Christological hymn in Philippians and its celebration of "Christ Jesus, who, though he was in the form of God, did not count equality with God a thing to be grasped, but emptied himself, taking the form of a servant, being born in the likeness of men. And being found in human form he humbled himself and became obedient unto death, even death on a cross" (Phil 2:5–8).

This experience of being saved by the love of God made manifest in Christ was made tangibly present for Saint Francis in two privileged ways: in the Eucharist and in the Bible.

The Eucharist, the *Poverello* believed and taught, was the royal road to the Father. By receiving the Body and Blood of Christ in the Eucharist, we become members of the Son, who alone fully reveals the Father of mercies. The Eucharist is the most tangible way in which the people of the Church become divinized. Thus the Eucharist must never be reduced to a matter of weekly or daily routine; the Eucharist, experienced as Saint Francis experienced it, should always be an occasion to be surprised by joy. Here, Francis anticipated the Second Vatican Council's teaching that the celebration of the eucharistic liturgy is the source and summit of the Church's life, and of every individual Christian's life.

Francis' love of the Bible as a way to receive the medicine of salvation was another anticipation of Vatican II and its restoration of the Scriptures to a central role in Catholic life; and here, too, is a Franciscan lesson for the Church of the twenty-first century.

To see the world through the world's eyes is to see things in a distorted way. Original sin was the original astigmatism, and in our time the *Kultursmog* of Gnosticism further distorts our perceptions of the human person and the human condition. But whatever the distinctive peculiarities of our moment, the problem of seeing things aright is a perennial one. That is what the Bible, read openly and, if you will, with Franciscan innocence, helps us to do. To see biblically is to see the world aright. Or, to vary the imagery, the Bible turns the world upside down so that the world comes into clearer focus.

The Christmas story, so familiar to us and so dear to Francis, is the beginning of this pattern of vision-correction-through-inversion: the Son of the Most High God, wrapped in swaddling clothes and laid in a manger. That pattern continues through the Gospels. Jesus doesn't evangelize the principalities and powers (although they, too, are welcome to listen and learn); he goes to the outcasts, including lepers and prostitutes, to announce and embody a kingdom in which Israel's God is king not just of the people of Israel, but of the whole world. Moreover, the Jewish Messiah will not establish God's rule and kingdom by political cunning, or by a display of worldly wisdom, or by knocking emperors and procurators off their thrones and judgment seats. He will reign from a different throne, an instrument of torture—the Cross. He will not be celebrated, like victorious Roman generals, with a triumphal spectacle conducted in the capital of a world empire. The signs of his triumph will be the pierced hands and feet of a transfigured, glorified body that defies time and space; burning memories of a conversation on the Emmaus Road; an empty tomb; a breakfast of grilled fish and bread on the lakeshore; a commission to go and convert the world, issued to a ragtag assortment of nobodies.

This biblical inversion of our ordinary perceptions and expectations, shaped as they are by the world's priorities, cures our astigmatism. Daily encounter with the Bible, especially the Gospels, allows us to see the world aright, as God sees it. To return again and again to the Scriptures takes us into the world of genuine happiness, which is the "inverted" world of the Beatitudes. Deep familiarity with the Bible enables us to penetrate the *Kultursmog* of the present and see things in the light of eternal reality and the divine gifts of creation and redemption.

Then there is the lesson for the twenty-first-century Church to be learned from Saint Francis the layman. While most scholars believe that Francis was ordained to the diaconate, his way of living the Gospel life was a decidedly lay pattern of the imitation of Christ, ordered to evangelization. Here we find in Francis an anticipation of Saint John Paul II's threefold teaching on the New Evangelization. First, all Christians, whatever their state of life in the Church or the world, are called to be missionary disciples. Second, the measure of our discipleship is our evangelical effectiveness in offering to others the gift of friendship with Christ that we have been given. And, finally, there are countless apostolates in which lay men and women will be the primary agents of evangelization, because those fields— the world of work and business, the media, the arts and sciences, politics—are arenas that laypeople properly formed in the faith are far more likely to penetrate than those in holy orders or consecrated life.

Saint Francis championed the Church's sacramental life, but the drama of his imitation of Christ took place in the world, not within the Church's sanctuary. His way of humility was available to all, whatever their state of life, which was why his example enflamed the spiritual imagination of the Middle Ages. And in this sense, he was the precursor of what *Lumen Gentium*, Vatican II's Dogmatic Constitution on the Church, described as the "universal call to holiness".

When I was a boy, I was given a book that I resurrected and reread a few years ago: *The Thirteenth, Greatest of Centuries*, by the now long-forgotten James J. Walsh. It's an all-stops-pulled celebration of the Middle Ages as the summit of Christian civilization—a sentiment I find at least somewhat attractive, until I remind myself that it would require later centuries for us to acquire the blessings of anesthesia, modern dentistry, and single-barrel bourbon. Yet, even if we lack James J. Walsh's unequivocal enthusiasm for medieval Christendom, H. Richard Niebuhr, in *Christ and Culture*, was surely right to say that the High Middle Ages witnessed the greatest synthesis of Christianity, culture, and society ever achieved. Nevertheless, the medieval synthesis was less than complete; the garment of the age was neither seamless nor unsullied.

Heresies proliferated during Francis' time: Waldensians, Cathars, Arnoldists, Humiliati, Patarines, Manicheans. Some of these off-brand movements were deeply confused intellectually. Others were groping down false paths toward the reform of an institutional Church that, for all its integration with culture and society, was becoming evangelically flaccid and sluggish, perhaps in the complacent conviction (not unlike that of the recent past) that the faith could be transmitted by cultural osmosis, as a kind of ethnic heritage. There were scandals of clerical corruption and simony. And there were other problems, chief among them the fact that, as one scholar puts it, "outside the monasteries and cathedrals, the religion lived and practiced by the faithful had been reduced to a collection of gestures and formulas, especially since the liturgical language—Latin in the West—had become unintelligible to them, and the priest was, above all, the man who knew and performed the efficacious rites."

In this situation, the medieval Church's most urgent challenge was mission: revitalizing the life of faith among those who were lukewarm, sparking faith in unbelievers, and transmitting the faith to the next generation. Francis sought to rekindle the evangelical fire in the Church by conceiving of Christian life not as a withdrawal from the world, but as a pilgrimage in the world, a pilgrimage toward and for conversion. The call to missionary discipleship was issued, Francis believed, to the whole Church, not just to clergy. By his own example, which was very "in your face", he jarred the Church of the thirteenth century out of its institutional comfort zone. He thus inspired new modes of Christian community that were essentially missionary in character, creating a new synthesis of the charismatic and institutional elements that are always present in the life of the Church. This caused a good bit of uproar, as parallel movements in our own time have done. But the uproar was contained, at least during Francis' lifetime, by his profoundly ecclesial sensibility and his evangelical obedience.

And that brings us to another Franciscan lesson for a Catholicism that, with other Christian communities, marked the five hundredth anniversary of the Lutheran Reformation in October 2017. Francis of Assisi was, without doubt, a reformer, even a radical reformer who sought to revitalize the Church through a reappropriation of its Gospel roots. But he was a reformer with a difference. As we ponder the quincentenary of the events in Wittenberg in 1517, it's good to remember the contrast between Francesco Bernardone and Martin Luther drawn by Georges Bernanos:

> One reforms the Church only by suffering for her; one reforms the visible Church only by suffering for the invisible Church. One reforms the vices of the Church only by multiplying the example of its most heroic virtues. It is possible that Francis of Assisi may not have been less disgusted than Luther by the lasciviousness and simony of the prelates. It is even certain that he cruelly suffered from them, for his nature was really different from that of the monk of Weimar. But he did not challenge iniquity; he did not try to confront it. He threw himself into poverty; he devoted himself to it to the deepest extent possible, as into the source of all remissions, of all purity. Instead of stripping away from the Church unjustly acquired goods, he showered it with invisible treasures and, under the gentle hand of this beggar, the mound of gold and wealth began to flower like a bush in springtime.

A Franciscan evangelical reform purifies the Church by returning to the eternal source of sanctity, Christ himself. That is the reform for which Pope Saint John XXIII hoped in summoning the Second Vatican Council. That is the kind of evangelical reform Pope Saint John Paul II sought to bring about by giving that council its authoritative interpretation. Saint Francis challenges us to put out into the deep of postmodernity, just as he challenged the complacent, "safe" Christianity of his own time. Catholicism today must leave the shallow and brackish waters of institutional maintenance, understanding that the Great Commission of Matthew 28:19 is addressed to each of us in baptism, and living the universal call to holiness in such a way that the world meets Christ in us—and thus meets the truth about itself.

Over the past half-century or so, too many parts of the Catholic world have come to think of "reform" as something we conjure up from our own cleverness, as if we must puzzle out what makes the Church relevant. Too often "reform" has been a matter of acquiescence, even surrender, to the spirit of the age. Perhaps Francis, who had a singular (and singularly intense) personality, experienced the temptation to think of reform, as some of our contemporaries do, in essentially Pelagian terms: as something we achieve by our own efforts and our own lights. One might find at least a tiny echo of this inadequate notion of reform in his initial impulse to rebuild Christ's Church by attending to ecclesiastical masonry—an episode in the early steps of his pilgrimage toward Christ that makes me think of present-day temptations to live the New Evangelization by getting top-drawer management consultants to advise the Church on messaging. But Francis came to see that renewal is always spiritual first, not institutional. He resisted the temptation to view things the other way around, and so should we.

All authentic reform in the Church recaptures and revitalizes the "form" that Christ gave the Church. That "form" is the Church's constitution (in the British sense of that word), what an older generation called the deposit of faith. We do not judge the deposit of faith, the Christ-given foundation of the Church; it stands in judgment on us and on our reforming efforts. And it is in retrieving lost elements of that constituting "form" and revitalizing them in our own time that we are true Catholic reformers. That was true of Vatican II's authentic reforms in its teaching on the nature of the Church, the office of bishop, and religious freedom. Forgotten or misplaced elements of the Church's Christ-bestowed constitution were retrieved and made the sources of Catholic renewal. That must be true of the ongoing work of reform in the Church today.

This was the mega issue beneath the issues at Synod-2014 and Synod-2015: the obedience of the Church to divine revelation, in which we find the Church's constitutive "form". The reality and binding character of revelation were a principal theme of Vatican II, where the key passage is paragraphs seven and eight of the Dogmatic Constitution on Divine Revelation, *Dei Verbum*. To imagine that

history, and especially ephemeral contemporary history, judges revelation is to put things precisely backwards. Doing so is what has cost
mainline Protestantism its vitality. That is not a road that the Catholic
Church should pursue; it is certainly not the road even so radical a
reformer as Francis of Assisi would urge us to pursue.

Francis prayed that he might be given the gift of suffering as Christ had
suffered, and his prayer was granted in the form of the stigmata—
another Franciscan *novum* in the history of the Christian spiritual life,
although it was anticipated in Paul's confession to the Galatians that
he bore on his body "the marks of Jesus" (Gal 6:17). The cruciform
participation in the suffering of Christ that Francis sought is now the
lot of millions of Christians around the world, who are violently persecuted for no other reason than that they are Christians.

We owe them a debt of solidarity on which we dare not default. In
addition to that, however, Catholics in the West today must understand that we are very likely heading into a season of persecution
ourselves, a season of the cross less dire than that lived by those Christians presently under direct mortal threat, but quite real nevertheless.
Our *Via Crucis* will not be as dramatic as that which unfolded in
ancient Mesopotamia in the first decades of the twenty-first century.
But it will be persecution, and it will extract costs: financial, social,
professional, and, likely, legal.

There are good reasons to mount challenges to the increasingly
aggressive intolerance and soft totalitarianism of postmodern progressivism. We owe our neighbors our best efforts to prevent further
diminishments of the common good. But we also need to adopt a
Franciscan disposition toward the coming challenges. That means
embracing persecution as more than the necessary cost of discipleship. Poverty was, for Saint Francis, the blessing of beatitude, for
it united him with Christ. Our cultural marginalization, even the
manhandling of our religious freedom by cynical uses of the law to
establish various orthodoxies of the sexual revolution, can be that
kind of Christ-conforming poverty for us.

If it comes to that, can we enter into this impoverishment of the
Church's status and influence in the West with a Franciscan spirit,
using our joyful embrace of Christ crucified and risen as an evangelical
opportunity to offer a death-dealing culture a path beyond its lethal

self-absorption and its confusion of the pleasure principle with beatitude? This distinctive, contemporary version of the marriage to Lady Poverty may well be the Franciscan task of the Church in the West at this historical moment. Embracing it, we may yet give the West a new birth of freedom, rightly understood.

# ACKNOWLEDGMENTS

Seven of these essays began as William E. Simon Lectures sponsored by the Ethics and Public Policy Center in Washington, D.C. So my first word of thanks must be to the William E. Simon Foundation, its board and staff, for sponsoring this annual lectureship. Thanks must also go to Sylvia Travaglione and all those on the EPPC staff who make the annual Simon Lecture work for all concerned.

Those of the essays that appeared in *First Things* and *National Affairs* benefited from the criticism and editorial deftness of Joseph Bottum, R. R. Reno, Yuval Levin, and Emily MacLean, whom I thank for their consideration and counsel.

Thanks, too, to my many hosts at Baylor University; to Dr. David Solomon for the invitation to Notre Dame; and to Father Alexander Sherbrooke for the invitation to speak at St. Patrick's in Soho Square, London.

Lauren Rae Konkol of the Ethics and Public Policy Center was invaluable in helping me get the essays into a form from which I could revise them for this volume, with a typically able assist from Stephen White.

Mark Brumley has been a persistent and valued friend, and I am delighted that his persistence has paid off in bringing this book to Ignatius Press, to which the English-speaking Catholic world owes a great debt of gratitude. Diane Eriksen saw the project through to completion with efficiency and good cheer. Thanks, too, to my literary agent, Nick Mullendore, for handling the arrangements.

It is a privilege to dedicate this book to two friends who were ordained bishops during the years in which these essays were prepared: Bishop Borys Gudziak of the Eparchy of St. Volodymyr the Great in Paris, and Bishop Robert Barron, auxiliary bishop of Los Angeles. Bishop Gudziak's work in establishing the remarkable Ukrainian Catholic University in L'viv, and in strengthening pastoral life among the Ukrainian diaspora in France, Belgium, the

Netherlands, Luxembourg, and Switzerland, has been a model of effective intellectual and episcopal leadership under the most challenging circumstances. Bishop Barron embodies the New Evangelization in the United States, and indeed throughout the world, in a singular way, and our work together with NBC News has been a joy. Turbulent times require stouthearted friends; this dedication is a small token of gratitude for the support I have received from each of these good men in my own work, and for the many important things I've learned from both.

G. W.
Washington, D.C.
October 22, 2017
Memorial of Pope Saint John Paul II

# NOTES ON THE ESSAYS AND SOURCES

The essays collected here have been revised, including emendations and additions, for this volume.

"The Great War Revisited" began as the thirteenth annual William E. Simon Lecture, delivered in Washington, D.C., on February 6, 2014. An edited version of the lecture appeared in the May 2014 issue of *First Things*. In preparing the lecture, I particularly benefited from, and cited material found in, David Fromkin, *Europe's Last Summer: Who Started the Great War in 1914?* (New York: Vintage Books, 2005); Christopher Clark, *The Sleepwalkers: How Europe Went to War in 1914* (New York: Harper, 2013); Sean McMeekin, *July 1914: Countdown to War* (New York: Basic Books, 2013); Max Hastings, *Catastrophe 1914: Europe Goes to War* (New York: Alfred A. Knopf, 2013); and Winston S. Churchill, *The World Crisis* (New York: Charles Scribner's Son, 1931). Each of these books provides a needed corrective to Barbara W. Tuchman's literarily masterful and influential, but analytically flawed, work, *The Guns of August* (New York: Bantam Books, 1980).

On March 23, 2010, I delivered the Laura B. Jackson Endowed Lecture in World Affairs at Baylor University in Waco, Texas. The edited lecture subsequently appeared under the title "Through a Glass, Clearly", in the August 2010 issue of *First Things*. The lecture's critique of typical American approaches to the morality and foreign policy debate drew on insights from "The Doctrine Is Dead", in John Courtney Murray, S.J., *We Hold These Truths: Catholic Reflections on the American Proposition* (Garden City: Doubleday Image Books, 1964).

"All War, All the Time" was the tenth annual William E. Simon Lecture, delivered in Washington on January 31, 2011, and later appeared in the April 2011 issue of *First Things*. Further information on the Communist war against the Catholic Church may be found in the second volume of my biography of John Paul II, *The End and the Beginning: Pope John Paul II—The Victory of Freedom,* the Last Years, the Legacy (New York: Doubleday, 2010); Christopher Andrew and Vasili Mitrokhin, The Sword and the Shield: The Mitrokhin Archive and the Secret History of the KGB (New York: Basic Books, 2001); and NKVD/KGB Activities and Its Cooperation with Other Secret Services in Central and Eastern Europe 1945–1989, Alexander Grúňová, ed. (Bratislava: Nation's Memory Institute, 2008).

"Grand Strategy Reconsidered" was the fourteenth annual William E. Simon Lecture, delivered in Washington on February 4, 2015, and later published in the May 2015 issue of First Things under the title "Lessons in Statecraft". Further information on John Paul II's approach to strategy may be found in three of my books: The Final Revolution: The Resistance Church and the Collapse of Communism (New York: Oxford University Press, 1992); Witness to Hope: The Biography of Pope John Paul II (New York: HarperCollins, 1999); and The End and the Beginning.

"Reading Regensburg Right" is based on a lecture delivered on November 30, 2007, at a conference, "The Dialogue of Cultures", organized by the University of Notre Dame's Center for Ethics and Culture. The full text of the Regensburg Lecture may be found at https://w2.vatican.va/content/benedict-xvi/en/speeches/2006/september/documents/hf_ben-xvi_spe_20060912_university-regensburg.html.

"Truths Still Held?" appeared in the May 2010 issue of First Things and was based on the ninth annual William E. Simon Lecture, held in Washington on January 28, 2010. The Murray template is adapted from my analysis of Murray's work in Tranquillitas Ordinis: The Present Failure and Future Promise of American Catholic Thought on War and Peace (New York: Oxford University Press, 1987), chapter 4.

"The Handwriting on the Wall" was the eleventh annual William E. Simon Lecture, delivered in Washington on February 7, 2012, and later appeared in the spring 2012 issue of National Affairs. A penetrating analysis of some of the deep sources of the turbulence in the contemporary West may be found in Henri de Lubac, The Drama of Atheist Humanism (San Francisco: Ignatius Press, 1995). Further information on Pope Leo XIII's analysis of political and social modernity can be found in Russell Hittinger, "Pope Leo XIII (1810–1903)", in The Teachings of Modern Roman Catholicism on Law, Politics, and Human Nature, John Witte, Jr., and Frank S. Alexander, eds. (New York: Columbia University Press, 2003), pp. 39–75.

"The Importance of Reality Contact" is based on the twelfth annual William E. Simon Lecture, delivered in Washington, on February 5, 2013, which later appeared under the title "Reality and Public Policy" in the spring 2013 issue of *National Affairs*.

"A New Great Awakening" was originally prepared as the sixteenth annual William E. Simon Lecture, delivered in Washington on February 1, 2017, and subsequently appeared in the spring 2017 issue of *National Affairs* under the title "A New Awakening". Further reading on "living in the truth" may be found in Vaclav Havel's essay "The Power of the Powerless", in Vaclav Havel et al., *The Power of the Powerless: Citizens against the State in Central-Eastern Europe* (Armonk, N.Y.: M. E. Sharpe, 1985).

"The Signs of These Times" is adapted from the preface to *Zeuge der Hoffnung: Johannes Paul II—Eine Biographie*, the German edition of my book *Witness to Hope*. An extended version of the preface appeared under the title "Blessed John Paul II and His Times" in the June 2011 issue of *First Things*.

An earlier form of "Synod-2014" appeared in the January 2015 issue of *First Things* under the title "Between Two Synods".

An earlier form of "Synod-2015" appeared as "What Really Happened at Synod-2015" in the January 2016 issue of *First Things*.

"Evangelical Churchmanship" was first delivered as a lecture at St. Patrick's Church in Soho Square, London, in October 2016 and later appeared in the January 2017 issue of *First Things* under the title "Franciscan Churchmanship". The analysis of Saint Francis is drawn from André Vauchez, *Francis of Assisi: The Life and Afterlife of a Medieval Saint* (New Haven: Yale University Press, 2012); G. K. Chesterton, *St. Francis of Assisi* (San Francisco: Ignatius Press, 2002); and Kenneth Clark, *Civilisation: A Personal View* (New York: Harper and Row, 1969).

# INDEX OF PROPER NAMES AND SUBJECTS

# INDEX OF SCRIPTURE